GODPRENEUR

Tapping The God-Principles
That Framed The Universe

Gbenga Mathew Owotoki

Dedication

To my Lord and Savior Jesus Christ. You are the reason why I live; you are the reason why I breathe. Thank you for making this possible.

To My Jewel of Inestimable Value, my best friend and dearly beloved wife, Eunice 'Rock Owotoki, thanks for your support, encouragement and prayers. You are the very best. Love you very much.

To my very own 'Pappi,' and Lemmy you both have brought fullness to my life, love you loads, sons.

Acknowledgment

A very special regards to my dear mother Mrs. Alice Owotoki who has been a strong pillar of supports. You set me early on the part of righteousness and labored constantly over me in Prayers. Love you loads. A big God bless you to the Pastors, Leaders, Workers and members of Mountaintop Faith International Church and Hephzibah Network International Ministries for all their support over the years.

A special thanks to everyone who have played one role or the other in my journey so far. I appreciate you and say God bless you richly

Preface

God is the greatest entrepreneur any human can ever think of. The wonders of the heavens and earth confirms He is incomparable He is never ending, a ceaseless pool of ideas and innovations. He is the fountain of life. I have never read neither have I been told about any successful entrepreneur that have never failed before but this is not so with God. There is no venture that he took up that never succeeded.

Beside the fact that He is God, there was a need that God saw -The earth was formless and there was darkness upon the face of the earth. He did not stop at seeing the need only but the 'Spirit of God moved.' It is not enough to see a need, you need to move to fill that need. This is one of the principles we will be expounding on as we read through this book and tap from God's own system. When we look at the scriptures and study carefully, we will discover that God was systemic when He created the world. We must understand that God saw the world as a product that needs to be created. The void and darkness presented a challenge but God saw through this a huge opportunity for something that has never been done before.

God knew what should be done, he was not beating around the bush like many of us; trying our hands in several businesses and not knowing exactly what we want. If there is a principle we must learn from God, it is the fact that God knew exactly what He wanted and He went for it. He saw a need, He worked on that need and as a result products were birthed.

Do you also realize that God did not create man before He created all that he did, in fact man was about the last of God's creation. This means God had a structure in place. The reason why your efforts hasn't paid off after several attempts could be because there are no structures on upon which your ideas can find expression. This is something you must learn to do.

Don't put the cart before the horse. God knew that creating man first will be a misplaced priority because there was no garden ready for the man to tend, there was no animal prepared for him to name etc.

This is a great lesson to learn. When you set out as an entrepreneur, don't allow your emotions becloud your sense of reasoning. Don't be overly excited as thoughts of projected profit run through your mind and as a result, you go blind on important structures which should have been in place. I have made these mistakes before and I have learnt a great deal of lessons from it.

I have no doubt that this book will open your eyes to the awesomeness and majesty of God and reveal to you on how we can connect with this endless Source of Power and ideas. With Him you can never go wrong. Have a pleasurable read and be blessed.

Contents

Chapter One: God – the Greatest Entrepreneur

Whether it is acceptable to our belief system or not, God is beyond the religious Names Christians associate Him with. Of course, He is Creator, Savior, Redeemer, Almighty One, Holy One, Righteous One, Healer, Provider, Refuge, Strong Tower and Everything to everyone. This therefore includes His being Entrepreneur, Investor, Innovator. Being the Omniscient One makes Him the Source of all ideas, inventions and even business acumen. Man's problem with the Image and Likeness doctrine is he views it from the reverse. He looks at himself and tries to draw a picture of God from what he sees in himself. The opposite is the truth. Man must look at God then align himself to the revelation of God of Who He is. Let's start from the very beginning.

¹In the beginning God created the heaven and the earth.

² And the earth was without form, and void; and darkness was upon the face of the deep. And the Spirit of God moved upon the face of the waters.

3 *And God said, Let there be light: and there was light.*

4 *And God saw the light, that it was good: and God divided the light from the darkness.*

5 *And God called the light Day, and the darkness he called Night. And the evening and the morning were the first day.*

6 *And God said, Let there be a firmament in the midst of the waters, and let it divide the waters from the waters.*

7 *And God made the firmament, and divided the waters which were under the firmament from the waters which were above the firmament: and it was so.*

8 *And God called the firmament Heaven. And the evening and the morning were the second day.*

26 *And God said, Let us make man in our image, after our likeness: and let them have dominion over the fish of the sea, and over the fowl of the air, and over the cattle, and over all the earth, and over every creeping thing that creepeth upon the earth.*

27 *So God created man in his own image, in the image of God created he him; male and female created he them.*

28 *And God blessed them, and God said unto them, Be fruitful, and multiply, and replenish the earth, and subdue it: and have dominion over the fish of the sea, and over the fowl of the air, and over every living thing that moveth upon the earth.*

Chapter One: God – the Greatest Entrepreneur

From the merchandising point of view, there was a need to be met. The earth was in total chaos. Order obviously is the need. And God moved to fill the need. He packaged order on the earth. His creation account even details the orderly fashion God made His moves. First day was light, fourth day was sun, moon and stars. He called them greater lights and lesser lights to rule day and night. Second day was separating waters above from waters below; fifth day was birds in the air above and fishes in the waters below. Third day was separating dry land from the waters and making plants grow. Sixth day was land animals and finally, man. Every need was met. God manufactured, so to speak, the earth as a product of perfection.

Meet the Need

God as Entrepreneur manifested the first principle of entrepreneurship – meet the need. This school janitor had worked the best years of his life with the owner who kept from everyone that his handyman was illiterate. It would definitely be an embarrassment for someone working in a school to not know how to read and write.

The owner died and his son took over. The son was not as sympathetic as the father and so when he found out the lack of educational qualification of the hapless groundskeeper, he fired him. The day he was thrown out of his job, the janitor walked aimlessly until he found himself in a part of the town he was not familiar with. He rummaged through his pockets for a cigarette or a piece of candy to allay his growing fear of being lost in the place he has never ventured into. He found none. He looked around for a place to buy these items but saw none. He walked from that street to another street and to several adjacent streets and discovered that the whole area does not even have a single store. He saw the need. With his separation pay, he rented a place in that area and put up a small cent and dime store. Being the only one in the area, of course the business prospered. Thence, he started looking for other areas that had no store in the vicinity and ended up with a chain of stores. When interviewed about his success, he simply said 'I needed something one day and found no store to meet my need. I imagined the other people who were in my predicament so I decided to fill that need with a store and another and another.' Thoroughly impressed the interviewer asked, 'Where did you learn that need principle you used?' The man nonchalantly replied, 'Nowhere. I cannot read or write.' Amazed more than before, the interviewer gasped, 'You were able to achieve all this as an illiterate! Where would you be if you had an education?' The man smiled, 'Still janitor of a school.'

The challenge was presented, the challenge was accepted and the man prevailed. After being declared as academically challenged, euphemism of unschooled, the man went right into overcoming the stigma through entrepreneurship. God of course was undaunted by the challenge of darkness and emptiness but similarly delved right into doing what has never been done before. The next principle God displayed was going ahead and doing it. The janitor did not dilly-dally. Without the benefit of an education to make the project study and projections and analysis, he just put in his savings before anyone else can discover what he found and beat him to the punch. God did not wait on anyone to counsel Him about the finer ways of creating things.

He just went and did it. Opportunity costs simply means not grabbing an opportunity presented until it is gone and cost you the windfall that never came. God in seeing the need knew exactly what He wanted to do and went ahead. The janitor saw the need and knew also what had to be done and succeeded.

Set the Structure

The other principle in entrepreneurship God's way is the setting up of a structure as foundational to the undertaking. Of course, the janitor had to scout for an open place he can rent at the proper location. God did start from ground up in His venture. The first obvious enterprise was to offset the darkness – Light be! From there layer upon layer atop each other were the other elements produced ready for consumer man. The janitor obviously dreamt profits as he stumbled on a gold mine of undertaking others overlooked but he built his empire one store at a time. He had hit on a formula worth repeating in every place crying out for the need. But he parlayed one success to another. The savings recouped from the first one became the seed for the next one and so forth.

Did it work? Was it good? An evaluation process must always determine the extent and time-span of the endeavor. The only indicator is the excellence of the merchandise. Anybody can produce anything; the best only produces the worthwhile. Genesis 1:31 declares: "And God saw everything that he had made, and, behold, it was very good. And the evening and the morning were the sixth day." God did not culminate creation with a passable earth; on the contrary, it had to be very good. Thus entrepreneurship God's way strives to present only the best and the very best; second-best is unacceptable. Mediocrity is damnable. Genesis 1:22 notes the first appearance of the blessing: 'Be fruitful and multiply.' The previous creatures of God were angels who had no reproduction in their system. On earth God introduces an innovation – life producing life. It was unique and never heard of. Entrepreneurship God's way must always present a distinct manner yet previously styled or an avant garde mode still unfashioned especially a method heretofore undiscovered to make life easier. God is both unhurried and consequently unrivalled in His development. He spoke birds, fishes and land animals into existence; He created man from dust and woman from man – a progressively marked improvement. God never shortchanges. Entrepreneurship God's way has no assembly line mentality churning out sub standard produce and service. Today's excellence is tomorrow's mediocrity. There will never be an end to improvement; when the best has been produced, something better is waiting to be made.

Timing is Perfect

Genesis 1:13 reads "And the evening and the morning were the third day." The very first noticeable fact is that nighttime precedes daytime. That's interesting! Yet, it is quite naturally what should be, since creation started with darkness before light came to be. In quite the same vein, setback gives way to success. The firing of the janitor from his job opened up the entrepreneurship long dormant in his uneducated visage. John would testify in his Gospel that darkness was not able to stop light from permeating and eventually dispelling darkness from its place. Likewise, entrepreneurship God's way guarantees throwing out lack and welcoming prosperity.

The same verse also brings forth the insight of dividing man's time relative to his activity. Day is for work and night is for rest, normally; but even the reverse of 12 hour shift for evening laborers would still clearly mark the time for employment and the time for setting aside the employ. This information further enlightens us to God's way of accomplishing His goals in a set deadline. What was to be achieved on the particular day was done and over with. The rest would wait for the next day. God shows focus even as the Almighty One into what is the daily limit of work to be accounted. The discipline of being able to direct the efforts to what is attainable at the workplace within the time frame is as important as the restraint of overworking self to death or divorce. The manager bringing home two suitcases of workload at home was met by the wife with these words," One suitcase brought home is devotion; two suitcases is adultery." It is never a measure of success that one overloads himself with toil; contrariwise, it is an indicator of unsound work ethic. There is only so much every man can hope to pull off in any given period. This adage greatly helps single-mindedness in the job. Since such-and-such needs completion then all faculties are employed towards the reaching of the goal. The remainder can wait for tomorrow. Thus, procrastination is eliminated. Cramming is eradicated. Today is today. Let tomorrow take care of own. Today's ideas must also find expression in its exactness. It is for the right time, the right moment; it cannot wait for the next day. Tomorrow's vision is precisely for that; but a day-to-day approach brings the steps closer to the dream. It does not remain a fantasy, it explodes into reality. Yet it is not a flash in the pan, here today and gone tomorrow; but a steady bringing about of the attainable through daily grind. God showed His mastery of creation as example. As God, He could have just brought all things together in a click of the finger. He did not. He was setting a model to follow. Entrepreneurship God's way is very realistic taking into view all these divergent stuff.

Nothing escapes God's good judgment. The timing is perfect. The execution is flawless. The order is immaculate. The priority is pristine. Closely imitating such example can certainly not lead to any epic fail. Then there is time to enjoy the vista, the panorama of the feat. Genesis 2:1-2:

[1]Thus the heavens and the earth were finished, and all the host of them.

[2] And on the seventh day God ended his work which he had made; and he rested on the seventh day from all his work which he had made.

Rest in Success

God never slumbers or sleeps. So, it is quite obvious that He never gets tired and does not need to rest. But His word testifies of the rest on the seventh day. In human terms, God instituted the no-work Sabbath for every man. He did also made it mandatory that even the land tilled should have a rest from producing year after year. It is then incumbent for the work force – man or beast – to take a break from back-breaking toil. Entrepreneurship God's way works best in a system that provides for ample time to rejuvenate the tired laborer to continue once refreshed. Rest also points to enjoying the fruits of the labor. For what does it benefit a man to sweat it out in diligent labor only for someone else to be the recipient of the harvest? It may sound commendable if the harvest was turned over generously. Wise King Solomon called it vanity. To him it was utterly useless and meaningless to exert all efforts only to see somebody else benefitting from all the hard work. At least have fun doing it; then fall back and relax because you have done it. James wrote that it should really be the farmer who should gain from the first fruits of his harvest before anyone else. Work only becomes truly rewarding not just because of the fulfillment in completion but also in reaping the dividends accumulated. Joy in fruitful endeavor is buttressed by more joy in the forthcoming gratification. For gratification may be delayed but should not be denied. Hardworking life becomes bearable in looking ahead to the leisure later available. Employment leads to retirement. Entrepreneurship God's way always end in lounging in comfort the rest of one's days.

Hebrews 4:10 adds another dimension to this thought. God ceased from His work as it continued – life begets life. Even the universe is still expanding after God rested. This ushers in the aspect of the continuance of what has been started. Entrepreneurship God's way operates with the principle of the work began not stagnating but expanding and multiplying. One store births another store. The two stores will birth another two stores, ad infinitum or saturation point. A soda drink in every house is the rallying call towards that endpoint. A Bible in every home is the outmost; unless the goal is spread farther into a Bible in every man, woman or child's hand. For apart from the family bible, each individual member has own copy of scriptures. Aside from family devotion, each family member schedules own time with God. Rest may be cessation of the entrepreneur from hands-on tough grind unto relaxation but the plugging away goes on unabated as the process progresses.

Chapter Two: Jesus – the Representative Entrepreneur

The fallacy of religious thought is that anyone can understand and make known to others the Incomprehensible, Inscrutable, and Invisible God by some form of self-consciousness in introspection and self-transcendence beyond bodily function through extended hours of self-denial looking deeper and deeper into the inner recesses of the soul or mindfully meditating on the wonderful sights of nature for after all such marvelous creation reveal the nature of God. All these so-called exercises fall short of the real unfolding of the truth of God.

The truth is in Jesus. He is the exact representation of the unseen God spoken about before time began.

Hebrews 1:1-4 J.B. Phillips New Testament (PHILLIPS)

1 1-4 God, who gave our forefathers many different glimpses of the truth in the words of the prophets, has now, at the end of the present age, given us the truth in the Son. Through the Son God made the whole universe, and to the Son he has ordained that all creation shall

ultimately belong. This Son, radiance of the glory of God, flawless expression of the nature of God, himself the upholding principle of all that is, effected in person the reconciliation between God and man and then took his seat at the right hand of the majesty on high—thus proving himself, by the more glorious name that he has won, far greater than all the angels of God.

Thus, a more perfect understanding of entrepreneurship God's way has to take a peek at the life of Jesus of Nazareth and how he walked in the principles of God as Entrepreneur. This is to showcase that such is attainable within man's grasp so that no one comes up with the excuse that the Almighty God can do it but man can just dream it.

Colossians 1:15-20J.B. Phillips New Testament (PHILLIPS)

Who Christ is, and what he has done

15-20 Now Christ is the visible expression of the invisible God. He existed before creation began, for it was through him that everything was made, whether spiritual or material, seen or unseen. Through him, and for him, also, were created power and dominion, ownership and authority. In fact, every single thing was created through, and for him. He is both the first principle and the upholding principle of the whole scheme of creation. And now he is the head of the body which is composed of all Christian people. Life from nothing began through him, and life from the dead began through him, and he is, therefore, justly called the Lord of all. It was in him that the full nature of God chose to live, and through him God planned to reconcile in his own person, as it were, everything on earth and everything in Heaven by virtue of the sacrifice of the cross.

God is Creator; Jesus Christ represents him as so. God is Entrepreneur; Jesus of Nazareth manifests him as so. To the plaintive plea of Philip to be shown God (Father), Jesus references himself as the point of knowledge regarding God (Father) as the only begotten Son.

John 14:8-14J.B. Phillips New Testament (PHILLIPS)

Jesus explains his relationship with the Father

8 Then Philip said to him, "Show us the Father, Lord, and we shall be satisfied."

9-14 "Have I been such a long time with you," returned Jesus, "without your really knowing me, Philip? The man who has seen me has seen the Father. How can you say, 'Show us the Father'? Do you not believe that I am in the Father and the Father is in me? The very words I say to you are not my own. It is the Father who lives in me who carries out his work through me. Do you believe me when I say that I am in the Father and the Father is in me? But if you cannot, then believe me because of what you see me do. I assure you that the man who believes in me will do the same things that I have done, yes, and he will do even greater things than these, for I am going away to the Father. Whatever you ask the Father in my name, I will do—that the Son may bring glory to the Father. And if you ask me anything in my name, I will grant it.

Note that in referring to himself, Jesus promises that anyone believing can accomplish entrepreneurship God's way. One has to believe that although God, Jesus lived his life a human being without distinct advantage over any other human being. Man works; Jesus was raised a carpenter's son and inherited that trade from his foster father before he launched into an itinerant preaching ministry. In both cases, he showed entrepreneurship learned from God (Father).

The inquisitive Phillip was subjected to an examination if he was astute enough for entrepreneurship.

Distributing Need

Here Jesus reprises entrepreneurship God's way. He saw the need. He asked Philip for a solution though he himself knew what he was to do. He was training a subordinate. Philip came up with an accurate financial picture. But he did focus on the seeming lack of resources not on a plausible solution. Now it is easy to crow 'miracle' and it has nothing to do with entrepreneurship. Without taking away from the fact that this is an actual miracle beyond the capacity of man, the execution draws a concrete idea of how entrepreneurship works. Remember the principle of order? Notice how Jesus instructed his disciples to set up a structure for easy distribution of the product – the five loaves and two fish. Entrepreneurship always must have a platform for distribution taking into account that no one area or consumers in that area should be lacking supply or impatiently waiting for orders to be filled or surreptitiously sent.

The distribution of the food in this case through orderly arrangement also made it easier to collect the leftovers. Jesus as exemplifying God (Father) set things in order. Distribution centers also serve as feedback for improvement. Interestingly after the feeding of the five thousand, 12 hand baskets were used to collect what was left; the next time in the feeding of the four thousand, 7 large baskets took up the leftover food. The disciples certainly learned from the first incident and were adequately prepared for the next.

Getting back to the executive reply of Philip, the group obviously had money. Jesus as CEO and COO had a CFO.

John 13:29-30J.B. Phillips New Testament (PHILLIPS)

28-30 No one else at table knew what he meant in telling him this. Indeed, some of them thought that, since Judas had charge of the purse, Jesus was telling him to buy what they needed for the festival, or that he should give something to the poor. So Judas took the piece of bread and went out quickly — into the night.

They had resources coming from diverse persons of different walks of life. They did have the finances to bankroll the enterprise.

Luke 8:1-3J.B. Phillips New Testament (PHILLIPS)

8 ¹⁻³ Not long after this incident, Jesus went through every town and village preaching and telling the people the good news of the kingdom of God. He was accompanied by the twelve and some women who had been cured of evil spirits and illnesses — Mary, known as "the woman from Magdala" (who had once been possessed by seven evil spirits) Joanna the wife of Chuza, Herod's agent Susanna, and many others who used to look after his comfort from their own resources. Unfortunately, the one with the money bag pilfered from the till and ultimately betrayed his head for thirty pieces of silver.

Notwithstanding this one bad egg, Jesus trained his disciples in ministry that can be used as principles in entrepreneurship 101. The goal is always change for the better. Old habits must be discarded; new ones adopted.

Minds are renewed by infusing novel thought processes. Yet though information is crucial to any form of learning, it is never an end in itself. Information with training leads to change. This involves actively engaging personnel in the process of life change.

Entrepreneurship Training

The very first lesson the disciples saw in Jesus was when he refused to be swayed by the crowd into their wishes. The customer may be right but it is up to the entrepreneur to present his product and not to be dictated upon by every whim and caprice even of the paying buyer. The downfall of any product would be trying to be everything to everyone when it has been specifically designed to meet the need but not all the needs. The Swiss knife has its limits. The mobile phone can only be utilized so much. Any product can only be as effective to its extent and never beyond what it is supposed to be.

The twelve was privy to this. The rest of the crowds could just get a glimpse of the person of Jesus as entrepreneur. Should the janitor-turned-entrepreneur in our illustration venture to have a thousand stores covering the biggest area possible he has to multiply himself so to speak. Every store as much as possible must be run by him or someone who has been trained to be like him. Training a thousand is not just formidable it borders on the impractical and improbable. The best the entrepreneur can do is to train ten who will in turn train their own ten training their own ten. District entrepreneurs will be under area entrepreneurs under the national entrepreneur. That takes time and the proper approach.

Foremost is the establishing of the relationship. Going back to God as entrepreneur, He treated Adam as a son to take over the entire operation. Looking to Jesus as entrepreneur, he commissioned the eleven to carry on the propagation of the product (the Gospel) into the outermost part of the earth starting from Jerusalem. God established His relationship with Adam, Jesus did exactly the same with his disciples. God spent the cool of the day with Adam; Jesus lived with his band of disciples taking them places as he trained them. The relationship was really basically for the disciples to listen and learn from Jesus plus to know him and be known by him. The affinity would even prompt two brothers to ask to be officially the External VP and Internal VP of the company much to the consternation of the other ten who also secretly wished for the lofty positions but were beaten to the punch by John and James (the sons of thunder as Jesus nicknamed them).

In his relational entrepreneurship training, Jesus used modeling. He showed the apostles whom he had chosen out of the multitudes following Him to be personally trained by Him how He does the Father's work. He lead by example and expected the twelve to do exactly the same. After being sent out two by two then returning successfully healing people and casting out demons, nine of these apostles got stuck for not being able to cast out a demon causing epileptic seizures while Jesus was at the Mount of Transfiguration with the other three. To the nine's plaint why they could not cast the demon out, Jesus very patiently replied, "This kind cannot come out except by praying and fasting." Very gently Jesus was reminding them that not because they have done it successfully should they now detached from the real

Source – God. He had shown them enough times that He would separate Himself from them for times of prayer with God. No amount of giftedness can compensate for losing connection with the Head. This is a very timely and timeless lesson for branches from the main office whose tendency is to adapt to their surroundings deviating from instruction from headquarters.

John 15:4-8 The Message (MSG)

4 "Live in me. Make your home in me just as I do in you. In the same way that a branch can't bear grapes by itself but only by being joined to the vine, you can't bear fruit unless you are joined with me.

5-8 "I am the Vine, you are the branches. When you're joined with me and I with you, the relation intimate and organic, the harvest is sure to be abundant. Separated, you can't produce a thing. Anyone who separates from me is deadwood, gathered up and thrown on the bonfire. But if you make yourselves at home with me and my words are at home in you, you can be sure that whatever you ask will be listened to and acted upon. This is how my Father shows who he is—when you produce grapes, when you mature as my disciples.

Chapter Two: Jesus – the Representative

The message is clear enough in branching out in entrepreneurship. The branch must do nothing unless authorized from the Head. This stems from the relationship developed between trainer and trainee that it becomes unthinkable for the trainee to act adversely from his trainer. The relationship aspect of entrepreneurship training is for the trainee to listen and learn, know his trainer and be known by his trainer.

In the instructional mode of entrepreneurship training, Jesus helped the learners think to find answers. They were quizzed and asked questions. They were allowed to ponder and ask what perplexed them.

Mark 8:14-21J.B. Phillips New Testament (PHILLIPS)

[14-20] The disciples had forgotten to take any food and had only one loaf with them in the boat. Jesus spoke seriously to them, "Keep your eyes open! Be on your guard against the 'yeast' of the Pharisees and the 'yeast' of Herod!" And this sent them into an earnest consultation among themselves because they had brought no bread. Jesus knew it and said to them, "Why all this discussion about bringing no bread? Don't you understand or grasp what I say even yet? Are you like

the people who 'having eyes, do not see, and having ears, do not hear'? Have your forgotten—when I broke five loaves for five thousand people, how many baskets full of pieces did you pick up?" "Twelve," they replied. "And then there were seven loaves for four thousand people, how many baskets of pieces did you pick up?" "Seven," they said.

21 "And does that still mean nothing to you?" he said.

They failed at this point to distinguish between physical and spiritual food; in entrepreneurship one must also be able to distinguish between what is effective from what is efficient and make the wise choice.

In His own interaction with them and the people, Jesus was consistently demonstrating to the twelve the proper handling of people and circumstances. Finally, He sends them for a field trip to interact with real life and real people without Him looking over their shoulders.

They successfully tackled the hands-on experience working independently of the Master yet dependent on the partner. Surely there was evaluation considering the effectiveness through feedback. The apostles reported everything they have done amazed themselves that diseases were healed and demons departed.

Finally, Jesus employed reflection as entrepreneurship training. The apostles had to deeply consider what they had learned and how they are to be applied.

His apostles could do more than the religious leaders. They have stood and shown themselves more powerful than these scribes in their flowing robes, but Jesus wanted them to focus on total dependence on God so called their attention to the destitute widow who has nobody else but God to turn to and gave all to God.

In this reflection they were also exposed to difficulties to manifest how they would react. In both instances involving storms in the sea the apostles exhibited fear even in the presence of Jesus. Jesus allayed the fears but also rebuked them in their baseless terror. After all, He was with them. Entrepreneurs must challenge themselves in different situations that may evoke panic if only to discover if they are apt to the task or will turn tail and run abandoning business and all.

In the final exposure to terror at Gethsemane and Calvary the mettle of the apostles was severely tested and found wanting. Resurrection however restored the apostles to their call.

Chapter Two: Jesus – the Representative

Chapter Three: God is into Serious Business

The point of all these is can God be trusted. Is He serious in His doing? Since He is Omnipotent is He just playing around knowing nothing can get past Him? Or beneath the loving kindness and patience and mercy is God fully committed to what He purposes to accomplish. Like an Entrepreneur bent on accomplishing what has been set not shirking from any obstacle walled along the path, God pushes on one day, a hundred day, a thousand years and more He keeps going on to the completion of what has long been set to happen.

In man, career paths take years and there must be a starting point. The first steps are truly challenging and results do not pour out as expected. People don't flock to a new business that has yet to be proven. People don't drive in droves to a product that has not been established as worth buying. There therefore the testing years. The wait-and-see attitudes of consumers are legend. Only the really adventuresome take the plunge. The rest wait to see if the pioneer keels over or benefits from the untested merchandise. Then they fall in line.

Hobbyists are not professionals. They just dabble amateurishly over a project and not take it seriously. Consequently they are not pushed to the limits of what can be achieved and sooner or later give up or settle on an armchair pleasantly viewing what has been achieved without imagining what more could have been done.

Their baby steps are erased by indecisiveness so they never break into a trot or sprint that should end up completing a marathon. They start again from the starting line and the finish line became as distant as when they first started. They keep negating what little headway they have made by not being challenged to develop seriously to endurance.

This dabbling with ideas one after the other is no way to building any sort of business entrepreneurship. Whether online or offline, such dabbling approach is utterly ridiculous considering that payoff only comes from consistency over a given period of time. Time is essentially to build a base of followers, attract consumers, develop merchandise and services, gain web links and search engine placements, generate other referrals, develop sound business sense, acquire adequate expertise, and intelligently figure out how to accrue income from work in ways that feel comfortable. It may take somewhere between two to three years to pass a target income for the really serious ones. Some may take longer. Semi-professionals give up after six months of no meaningful income and try another gig. They do not have the patience to see through something worth keeping up with. When they give up too easily they never reap the benefits waiting in long-term mode. Short-term goals must be added on one on top the other to reach the long-term prospect. The first short-term goal may be for only such and such income. The next short-term goal will not be unrealistically double the first. It must be a percentage higher but not stagnation. One per cent increase is still increase. Weak financial results during the first tries are not indicative of the long haul. But one must stay the course to eventually see the coming downpour of finances. Such goals parlayed one after the other should show a pattern of sustainable growth. At least don't give up until you glimpse the pattern.

The dabbling stage is the experimental phase exploding to actual mass production. The prototype can still be improved on, overhauled and reset from scratch. But it has a purpose. The main purpose is to move from dabbling to actually producing. The target to generate serious income and enjoy an abundant lifestyle is crucially linked to getting past the dabbling phase. Incessant dabblers are perpetually broke if not perennially frustrated. They keep giving up on themselves and changing their minds well before they could have already otherwise begin reaping the long-term benefits of sustainability and growth. Before they could even have a chance to experience serious results, they inadvertently pull the plug and washes down the drain all the hard efforts done.

The indisputable fact is that serious income can be had from just about any form of work creative, technical and everything in between. Writing and translation, audio and video production, arts, music, programming, design, information technology, computer aided design, transcription, and a hosts of others. Many have traversed these paths and have made a decent living. Still others who came before have already made millions from these endeavors. Most of the successful ones didn't get very far in their first 6-12 months. The ones who stuck with it for more than five years started reaping the biggest benefits. They're builders, not dabblers; winners not quitters.

There is a singular pattern patent in the most successful hobbyists-turned-professionals. They all got to the crossroads of continuing dabbling or dropping everything and get serious. They all made that decision to be serious from that point onwards. They determinedly decided to stop dabbling, stop drifting, and stop coasting. They got committed to one particular path and doubled down on it, intending to stick with it for as long as it takes in man-years so they could really master the work. Consequently, these people unlike the rest are now enjoying serious results. Meanwhile, the dabblers left behind are still looking for that next Get Rich Quick idea they hopelessly hope can grant similar results within a matter of months.

If close friends are asked what kind of work you'll be doing 5 years from now, how will they react? To be absolutely sure, quiz them. When their answers are inconsistent, off tangent from each other and confusing, then wonder why? How do these guys perceive you? Do they see a wishy-washy dabbler, a happy-go-lucky wishful thinker, a non-committal pursuer of dreams? A committed person broadcasts self as such. It is must not just be crystal-clear to the individual but obvious to the group he runs around with that he is one committed do-gooder. They certainly would want to be around someone ready to make a stand for what he believes and not have cold feet at anytime. The ones projecting strong presence on a strong and successful pathway can easily be predicted as being this or that person after just five years. People around this person can clearly surmise the arena he is mastering. It is the area he is putting it all right this very moment.

Stick-to-itiveness is a basic barometer pointing towards abundant income rivers and streams leading to enjoying the long-term benefits one's passion. The interest whatever it is must be something that has been brewing in the heart and will remain sizzling for more years to come. Make sure to stick the finger to the very core of the interest since tangent ideas, congruent clues and indicative notions may coast along side-by-side complementing the main interest. But the core remains the core. The rest come alongside for a time, boost the passion, and even spur spurts of excitement yet everything is assuredly anchored on this one thing to be done. The choice is foremost. The choice must be correct. Should it be something not really one's passion, it will eventually fade to nothingness and will not be pursued as ardently.

Fleeting interests are just that. They flee. They don't stay. They are fair-weather ideas that won't stand challenges along the way. Career paths are laid by serious commitment to a singular inspiration. All others are clouds floating away and will not stay put. Childhood interests that are magnified in teen years and looked deeper into during young adulthood are more surely the career path to be taken. Then there are second careers. The boyhood dreams may have now faded or have already reached fruition; there is still more. As the years go by, what other interests keep cropping up even when engrossed with another undertaking. This might very well be the second career after the culmination of the first. Are you still game? It might even have been the original just set aside or covered by the one considered seriously since reason came to being in one's life. It's not too late; it's a second start after the first success.

Doing something over and over again for an extended period does not qualify as committed to mastery. Most males are into weekend sports but will never be professional athletes raking in millions. Other males are into weekend warriors but will never volunteer for overseas duty facing real bullets. They may have been at it since puberty, but they never reached maturity. They never intended to. That's fine. It remains a hobby but not a source of significant income. Consequently, it is unwise to challenge a master when you have remained an amateur. The skills are elementary not exemplary; the stance is mediocre not excellent. The result is hogwash. There is no improvement; there never will be. It is just dabbled during weekends. It is not taken up seriously.

Since you consider being half-way there as the tone of your career, then there is absolutely no reason to strive for mastery. The consequential result is taken with a grain of salt. The die is cast this is how far you go. Someone okay being no better off in a career 5 years from now has no real need to commit to mastery. They just keep dabbling, or doing what they've been doing without making a serious commitment. But if one is the other kind to whom it's not very palatable to stagnate and longs for stronger results 5 years from now, then it's time to consider getting very, very serious.

Dabbling for experimentation or for the sake of exploration is acceptable to a certain point. It's fine but it is not a chosen career path. It is embarrassingly sounding foolish to broadcast that every 6 months the career path has changed yet again. What is being experimented on and being explored upon are avenues of learning – no more, no less. Going beyond experimentation and exploration leads to building something that endures and won't be quitted after just a few years; it is it!

Principle to live by

Anything that can be committed to seriously for just less than a year is not a career path. God's commitment is for eternity.

Biographies of very successful men and women highlight one theme frequently surfacing – these people have a strong inclination for concrete action. Those who seek to achieve high levels of success in absolute areas of life tend to take a lot more action than those who settle for average or below average results.

Almost all people come up with interesting ideas to pursue. Everyone probably comes up with some great ideas while going about the mundane day. But very often when an idea present itself as actionable, it fades away, people are talked out of it, it is overcomplicated and dies on the vine not allowed to see the light of day, This is not the typical action of most successful people. They are more likely to take action — either right away or shortly after they engender the cool idea.

The vote for inaction

It is so easy to neglect taking the proper first step at the birth of an idea. The first misstep is to lose focus. The coolest idea crops up, but instead of staying focused on it, one is distracted from it. Instead of making the new idea a top priority, attention is mysteriously switched to something else. This withdrawal of focus makes the idea obscured. It becomes fuzzy. The enthusiasm initially showed fades out as in a drama. The mental RAM gets overwritten. Sooner or later, the once cool idea cools off and eventually forgotten.

One can even argue self out of an idea that came to the same person's mental self. Instead of assent, doubt comes questioning the very foundation of the idea. The focus shifts to the opposite. The idea is not workable. It might lead to failure. Whatever can go wrong will go wrong (Murphy's Law). The unseen problems are brought to fore obfuscating the endless possibilities including the opportunities. The once brilliant idea loses its luster. It becomes less and less attractive. Eventually, the conclusion is made that the idea will bring more trouble than it ought and becomes rejected, relegated to the garbage bin of lost dreams.

Others will also gladly accommodate one's misgivings. Their questionings essentially are internalized paving the way for rejection of the illustrious idea. You can also allow others to talk you out of your idea. This is essentially the same thing because you must internalize their attitudes in order to kill the idea.

Lastly, there is overcomplicating which is the exact opposite of oversimplification. Instead of remaining faithful to the core, more complex features are added expanding the idea to a monstrosity indistinguishable from the original. It grew to be so grandiose that there is no way to launch it in properly and implement it in a reasonable period of time. Perfectionists are the prime proponents of this doing it more often than most. Implementations that are "good enough" (though not mediocre) can still provide a lot more value than doing nothing, but when the launch is overcomplicated, inaction becomes the more attractive choice.

The mental processes of evaluating and re-evaluating are not *wrong* per se, but the long-term consequence is that running any of these subroutines will inevitably lead to avoiding taking definite action most of the time with an interesting idea. These thought processes favor maintaining the status quo because they derail the implementation of new ideas.

Maintaining the status quo is a viable option and very important to some. It is quite reasonable to stick to it from time to time; but there are consequences. Applying such processes to life inordinately makes one lose sight of golden opportunities. The potential advantage is that it avoids making errors of commission. Inaction naturally disposes of new failures and rejections caused by costly mistakes.

The affirmation for action

With an interesting idea, the tendency is for the focus to naturally flow into specific action. Instead of letting other thoughts get in the way, the schedule is set to stay with the idea and see where it leads. Elevating the status of spontaneously cool ideas in life invariably takes precedent over maintaining the status quo. When struck by an inspired idea, everything else is dropped in favor of running with the idea to where it leads.

One can always talk self to take appropriate action based on the idea. Attention on the possibilities of what might work as opposed to the potential problems is articulated. The upside is more pondered on than the downside. Others may chip in their two-cent worth to prod further into the needed action. Companions who love to push to the edge are distinct advantages at this point.

Finally, simplifying the idea for easier takes is brilliant devised. The actions to be taken are more accessible and easier to undertake if just focused on the core essence of the idea. The intermediate subsidiaries can be tackled later on.

The choice is this or the other – action or inaction. Though inaction can be useful at certain stops; action is the fire starter. More projects can be stirred into being. The challenges of fiasco and letdown are met head on instead of being waited upon to hit the project.

Chapter Three: God is into Serious Business

Which line of attack is better?

Inaction is a line of attack; it is a viable stratagem. Action is also an advance to what is hoped to be achieved.

Should one feel life is about 95% accomplished, why risk it for the remaining 5% that is sure to come having reached this far? There is no other option but inaction! Maintaining the status quo relieves undue pressure. The momentum is already there. There is not stopping towards the goal, why change gears at this stratum? It is foolhardy! It is insane to take action at this juncture. It is wiser to coast long the victory enjoying the effortless ride. Why throw away happiness for an uncertain new action that may end up unfulfilled? There is a later, a much, much later.

On the other hand, those ambitious for farther and further growth should not stop even for a moment. (Smelling the roses by the wayside is for later!) New experiences wait. Maintaining current situation should give way to creating something new. The status quo can be shaken to take a pot shot at something seemingly better. Faster and faster action must be engaged. Catastrophes and collapses are small prices to pay so as not to let a golden opportunity slip through the fingers. Better to cry over spilled milk than never to have seen the milk.

Someone muttering too often the following catch phrases should slow down: "I really wish I hadn't…" or "How could I have done something so stupid?" or "I should have thought that through more carefully"? Haphazard deeds are hazardous in the end. Pause and take deep breaths before moving on. Be circumspect. Be more deliberate in the next steps. Don't bit more than can be chewed.

The other catch phrases point towards the other direction: "Why didn't I jump on that opportunity when I had the chance?" or "I wish I'd signed up for that years ago" or "I'm feeling behind relative where I think I should be at this time in my life"? Action bias mode must be geared on! Speed up and be more spontaneous. Forget the torpedoes! Dive on!

In reality, both are equally needed. There is a time to act as there is a time to not act. Both are equally important in life. It is not vacillating from one process to the other. It is wisely discerning which is more beneficial for the moment. Action from rapid change comes and slows down; coasting along can't last for long and must be prodded to speed things up.

Mixing and matching these two divergent styles is also vital specially applied to different aspects of life. Social life may be on the go while the intellectual life coasts along. Physical exertion may lie dormant while rest is enjoyed. Upgrading one may really call on the maintaining the other as is.

Pacing self according to the exertion is tantamount to denying involvement in the rat race of nothing but busy schedules without a breather. That is not top of the hill; it is rock bottom in temperance. A change of pace at decent intervals rejuvenates everything needed to keep up in the race ahead.

But the Biblical principle is to speak what you believe and have what you say. So, what comes out of your mouth is what develops in your life. The entrepreneurship follows the thoughts not kept in the mind but expressed by the tongue.

Forever Consequences

Very few people really consider eternity in entrepreneurship. Our focus sadly is only for the here and now. God is eternal He favors every action taken or words unspoken has bearing with forever. God has no short-term or long-term concepts. He is always Today which is eternity past and eternity future existing in the present.

Unfortunately, finite man is into such chronology. Short-term, mid-term, long-term betray the ineptness of man's ability placed side-by-side with Omniscient grace. So, man moves with short-term fluctuations in action averaging out over time. The median balances out the weeks of feverish action with weeks of indulgent inaction. In the long haul, what is more prevalent? Individuality bears this out. Circumstances also have a lot to say.

The long-term concept advocates whether one is more inclined to action or biased towards inaction even if both are quite manifesting subsequently in everything done or not done. It seems although a balance is ideal; it is persisted that one is either or the other. Shall we call it an action figure that slows down from time to time or a pensive thinker that springs to action ever so often when called to? Should there really be a dominant trait? Is there really a pattern? Is it really the norm of successful men and women to be jumping about endlessly moving in perpetual motion so as to be adjudged and acclaimed as earth-shakers and world-changers and society-movers? So, is there no usefulness to the silent thinkers, the Walden Pond types who refuse to be drawn to such prodigious activities and miss the beauty of every inhale and savory intake of delicacies?

Some maintain it shouldn't be too difficult to see why very successful men and women tend to have a strong bias in favor of action. They purportedly lean in the direction of focusing on their new ideas, looking at the positive possibilities, and talking themselves into action. The question still remains: Is it absolutely reasonable to favor action though? Wouldn't it be better to spend more time deliberating and thinking things through carefully? This haply depends on what is being worked on. Launching a NASA mission meticulously entails to triple-check everything to make sure it's safe. The consequences of failure can be very extremely high in trillions of dollars and cost of lives. Doubtless, in cases where the consequences of failure aren't fatal, like risking some embarrassment or a break-up or a bankruptcy, well... that may sting a little, but recoverable. Does God think so? Does God miss the detail for the big picture?

Motivators ask the pointed question: "What are the realistic worst-case consequences if my idea fails to work?" They aver that in many cases it has to be admitted that in the grand scheme of things, the negative consequences just aren't a big deal. To those who may make them a big deal in their minds, but are people going to lose their lives if one makes an honest mistake? (But they do!) Taking action is rarely fatal these days according to some. They can screw up a lot, recover, and keep right on going. Not with God, every mistake has a consequence eternally shared. A simple eating of the forbidden fruit spelled doom for millions forever. That's no small consequence.

Unmitigated action does not necessarily result in greater long-term success. Eating the fruit (inaction) would have maintained the blessing not brought in the curse.

The collective thinking is that lots of action invites a tremendous amount of experiential learning. Thus experience becomes the best teacher. Learning from the mistakes of others seems to be the better route. Why not let the other guy make the mistake and learn from it? Why insist on making your own mistake then crow about learning something after hitting the dust face first? While it is true that we can learn a great deal from books and teachers and coaches but we must still learn certain things from experience, the Word of God is God's way of actual teaching not circumstances foisted on us by the world instigated by the god of this world.

Truth is there are skills to be learned in actuality specifically physical movements like walking, talking, dancing; but lest we forget there are principles behind these movements that explain why these action are possible.

Importune action like driving a car may seem to just need action. Such wrong mentality has caused death and accidents. All these drivers care about is getting into a car and get started not assuming the responsibility of keeping safe the passengers, other drivers and pedestrians. The jump-into-action entrepreneur totally ignores driver education as vitally important before even turning the ignition keys on. Peer pressure does talks teenagers into the freedom to come and go as it pleases them not regarding the dangers of joy riding and total wreck of the parent's car.

This is not to condone inaction. The idea is not to maintain the status quo of being a non-driver but the responsible action of being an educated driver and not an irresponsible entrepreneur. For the principle works likewise in entrepreneurship; inaction does inure self to making mistakes and failures (errors of commission) as well as deny picking up valuable skills and getting involved in more opportunities. Action mode on the other hand does increase opportunities and totally obliterates errors of omission. Erroneously it is espoused that missing opportunities hurt the results in the long run. This is patently Satan's lie in the garden. It was quite clear that the serpent deceived the woman in believing that God was withholding the golden opportunity to possess the knowledge of good and evil. The biggest failure is not the failure to act but the failure to act responsibly. God is a responsible Entrepreneur.

Change is inevitable. Even death does not mean a cessation of change for man still changes to dust. Embracing change is not the challenge; resisting evil change is. This is where inaction will prove fatal; but to actually be moved by every wind of doctrine, running wild after every change is courting disaster. Indeed not all change is positive that is why both action and inaction must be discerning of what is best employed. It is not to avoid virtually every change and thus miss golden opportunities, it is to be wise into lessening risks by taking only the change that are beneficial and avoiding the rest. Calculated risk with the guidance of God does not avoid positive results but more likely guarantees such. The low-hanging fruit should have satisfied Adam and his wife, the fruit in the middle of the garden was not to be accessed. Change in the garden was definitely not an improvement.

Moving forward through action/inaction

Ideally actions must lead to success; it is perfectly sane to avoid taking actions that lead to failure. This is a no-brainer. However, inaction is as ideally also a path to achieving and maintaining success. The best ideally is a combination of action/inaction. The Israelites of old crossing the wilderness were taught this way; the Shekinah glory lifts, they move; the Shekinah glory settles, they stop. It wasn't all moving forward, it was stopping from time to time. The Sabbath was established primarily for that. These Egyptian slaves were in perpetual motion serving their taskmasters dawn to dusk daily without fail. God had to re-condition them into inaction at least once a week. Those who could not resist action ended up with nothing for their labor; one even paid for his life for bias towards action.

Since even the best opportunities tend to be unpredictable, inaction is a perfect foil for non-stop action. Reducing risks to guarantee success includes waiting for the most opportune time to act which means inaction for the time being. There really is no applicable formula to eliminate uncertainty; there is a hibernating period to make things more certain. Randomness is a mitigating factor; waiting upon the Lord is the antidote. Since the world under the sway of the evil one wants man injured without rhyme or reason and the thief only comes to steal, kill and destroy and man cannot declare it is a no-fault clause, there must be a defense not to leave us helpless. God has. Every entrepreneur should know that.

No action should be taken without guidance from God thus eliminating doubt. God does not work with the evil heart of unbelief; faith pleases God. Any entrepreneur's action without faith is purposely missing the mark.

It is not just unwise to be reckless; entrepreneurship God's way precludes any action not directed by God. The odds do not have to be in one's favor; God has to be for and not against the action or inaction as the case may be. Success or failure or anything in between is not to come as expected. God never fails. Hearing God and obeying Him guarantees success all the time every time.

An action bias does not become a long-term advantage simply because the more one takes action; the more is learned about risk. Inaction is also taking risks of missing the boat. Action cannot make one an expert in developing a better feel for how to tell when the odds are favorable.

Trial and error is what is resorted to by those not in the habit of reading the Bible and praying every day. It is a slow and tedious process, and not the fastest way to learn. Humans are capable of single-trial learning; believers are graced to hear from God. It is not necessary to repeat mistakes to learn to avoid them. One bad experience can teach one to avoid specific problems for the rest of one's life. Sometimes a mistake is done and by God's grace never repeated. The lesson has been learned in a matter of seconds.

Both action and inaction gain feedback. Not doing anything will elicit comment. Doing something will also invite criticism. It is not as if you fail to take action, what might have been haunts. Second-guessing God is never a good habit. Neither is que sera sera – whatever will be will be. This is not fatalistic plunge head-on. It is faith in an Almighty God who intercedes and intervenes for the good of those who love Him and are called to entrepreneurship. Action limits growth of an improvement when going the opposite direction. Inaction limits potential and progress by standing still. Favoring action gains the long-term benefits of action-based feedback. In the long run, these benefits can be massive. Favoring inaction also gains benefits of knowing when to pull back and watch God move. When perusing lot of biographies of highly successful men and women, see how critical action-based feedback is. There aren't many stories where people set a clear goal and achieved massive success right away. Success came as a result of refinement over many years and decades including times of intermittent inaction.

Take action. Observe. Make the adjustments. Take another stab at it. Lay back and take hands off for a while. Most of the time, the first stab will fail. So will the second and the third. Eventually through much prayer it's figured out. Actually, it would have been figured out earlier if bathed in lots of prayer. It does save from grief of several puny tries. Sometimes it can't be figured out though. It is time to recoup. There are really no faith failures. It is extremely bad habit to recommend faith experiments to fail and be tried again. Faith cometh by hearing and hearing by the Word of God; no word, no faith, no action should be taken.

Persistence

Trial and error is the luxury of the young; yet most young entrepreneurs want massive positive results without going through that long-term process learning and leaning on the Lord. Many of them have a low tolerance for failure; they give up easily. They see persistence only as far as a year tops. This is still amateurish dabbling without serious commitment.

The bumps in the road are inevitable especially if one is not attuned to the principles and programs of the Entrepreneur God. Unfortunately when people ask about success, they're mainly looking for techniques and tactics and tricks. What methodology can they apply to achieve similar results? Apart from prayer and the word as led by the Spirit, techniques are personally achieved. It differs from one Christian to the next. What has been set in the heart of one for years cannot be duplicated by another even for the same number of years.

Ephesians 2:10 Amplified Bible (AMP)

For we are His workmanship [His own master work, a work of art], created in Christ Jesus [reborn from above — spiritually transformed, renewed, ready to be used] for good works, which God prepared [for us] beforehand [taking paths which He set], so that we would walk in them [living the good life which He prearranged and made ready for us].

God's commitment is everlasting; man can do no less. What is being measured today in finite years has infinite bearing for eternity. A century is infinitesimal compared to forever.

Eternal Commitment

Man's thinking including his planning is limited by eons – time frames. His commitment is likewise that myopic. It is the main reason why average and below average results are more common than exceptional results. Looking forward to a couple of decades does not cut it. Everything done must be with an eye to the everlasting.

Most people aren't going to commit to this. Christians are already committed to eternal life in Christ. Therein lays the greatest advantage. Something that is forever can be perpetually adjusted to with the never-ending hope of betterment. Today is not the best day ever. This life is not the best life now. Forever is still waiting with the promise of life getting better.

The field may look crowded, but that's most likely because it's flooded with dabblers. They'll be gone within a year or less, replaced by newer dabblers. These people don't represent any serious competition, at all. In fact, they're most likely helping without even knowing. They'll introduce new people to the field (an advantage to those who remain!) before they eventually give up. Think of these dabblers as unwitting volunteer marketing team. They help to expand the market for the products and services that the ones that outlast them eventually deliver.

Psalm 139 is a must read for those thinking of what has been set since childhood. Applying it to an individual today is quite natural (even to non-Christians it is supposed). Steve Wozniak, as an example, started learning about electronics when he was about 4 years old (his Dad was an engineer who worked on missile programs), and he was winning science fairs and building computers while in grammar school. Building the first Apple computer was the result of a progression that began many years earlier from childhood.

Commitment doesn't mean trapping or limiting self as it is a bad idea to limit God in what He wills and can do. It's not about putting self in a box or a cage. It's about choosing a certain line of development and running with it, which isn't that difficult to do when one discovers something God has anointed the believer with. Naturally, man starts to love God's plans for him since it came from God who loves him. Then the commitment is a commitment to God who wants the believer to enjoy life and to express what feels good to God and to him. It cannot be apart from God, His word, His plans and His ways. It's still going to involve a lot of work, but that work is mostly a labor of love, God working in the believer His good pleasure. The question is whether or not the Christian yields his life to God surrendering all and willing to put in the miniscule time on earth to set eternity in motion in this life.

Lean into God's promises without doubting. Doubts are of the devil to stop progress forward. It's unreasonable to expect perfect clarity in advance. It takes faith and faith is not in the realm of reason. It does take spiritual exercise to hear the slightest whisper of God but the Holy Spirit was sent to reveal even things to come. A faint idea is good enough. Take baby steps to prevent headlong fall. Keep moving towards that direction ever attentive to the leading of the Spirit.

God plants the seed, the word. Thus it is incumbent to spend time in the word for the seeds to be planted. Meditation and prayer waters the seed to grow one doesn't even know how.

Mark 4:26-29 Expanded Bible (EXB)

26 Then Jesus said, "The kingdom of God is like someone who plants seed in[scatters seed on] the ground. 27 Night and day, whether the person is asleep or awake, the seed still [sprouts and] grows, but the person does not know how it grows. 28 By itself the earth produces grain. First the plant [blade; stalk] grows, then

the head, and then all the [the ripe] grain in the head.[29] When the grain is ready, the farmer cuts it [with a sickle], because this is the harvest time."

Chapter Four: God's Entrepreneurial Keys

Perfect Partner

Proverbs 19:14 Expanded Bible (EXB)

14 Houses and wealth are inherited from parents, but a ·wise [insightful] wife is a gift from the Lord.

God created the ultimate help-meet. She was to partner with the man to fulfill the mandate of dominion and authority, filling the earth with like-minded offspring and being fruitful and multiplying overall starting from the Garden. The commanded blessing has not changed. God commanded blessings forevermore. A partner spouse is mandatory.

She is to be included in every major decision. One marriage guru even suggests – she's the Holy Spirit stand-in. 'Listen to your wife!' should not be taken as contrary to what Adam heard – Because you listened to your wife – then the curses came. Give and ear to the godly wife who also does her devotions consistently and her prayers fervently. Peter warned that the husband's prayer is hindered when the wife is not treated properly. Amidst the busyness of the entrepreneurship, make family time and regular vacations a priority. Bonding is effective and efficient as to the juncture of getting to be more acquainted with each other. "I never knew you can do that!" The admiring thrill in the probably high-pitched voice of the good wife says it all. The palpitation within the husband's heart is profoundly priceless. The good wife knows there are more treasures to be unearthed. She believes there is more drama and interest in her somewhat portly husband than the latest million best sellers or box-office shattering movies. But the distinct unearthing is not the result of reworking the mate it is the result of trusting a compassionate good wife. Beneath the surface, lies the undiscovered husband who is a perfect complement to the good wife. It takes a good wife to bring the masterwork of GOD to the wide open. It takes a good while to bring the progressing process to its fruition. It takes an entire lifetime that is why vows call for staying together until death. And before the inevitable parting sets in the discoveries about each other has mounted to mountains of information. Thus, seeking advice from the spouse is being sure she has something worthwhile to suggest.

There's a charming story that Thomas Wheeler, CEO of the Massachusetts Mutual Life Insurance Company, tells on himself. He and his wife were driving along an interstate highway when he noticed that their car was low on gas. Wheeler got off the highway at the next exit and soon found a rundown gas station with just one gas pump. He asked the lone attendant to fill the tank and check the oil, and then went for a little walk around the station to stretch his legs. As he was returning to the car, he noticed that the attendant and his wife were engaged in an animated conversation. The conversation stopped as he paid the attendant. But as he was getting back into the car, he saw the attendant wave and heard him say, "It was great talking to you." As they drove out of the station, Wheeler asked his wife if she knew the man. She readily admitted she did. They had gone to high school together and had dated steadily for about a year. "Boy, were you lucky that I came along," bragged Wheeler. "If you had married him, you'd be the wife of a gas station attendant instead of the wife of a chief executive officer." "My dear," replied his wife, "if I had married him, he'd be the chief executive officer and you'd be the gas station attendant."

Competent Counselors

Ecclesiastes 4:9-12 Expanded Bible (EXB)

9 Two people are better than one,

because they get ·more done by working together [a good return for their hard work/toil].

10 If one falls down,

the other can help ·him [his colleague] up.

But it is ·bad [a pity] for the person who is alone and falls,

because no one is there to help.

11 If two lie down together, they will be warm,

but a person alone will not be warm.

12 ·An enemy [Someone] might ·defeat [overpower] one person,

but two people together can ·defend themselves [stand up against them];

·a rope that is woven of three strings is hard to break [a three-stranded cord does not quickly snap; C having a friend is good, having more friends is better].

Of course, the faithful members of the best company are those who are bent on having the entrepreneur's best interest firmly embedded in their hearts. Otherwise, bad company corrupts good morals. They are wont to ask not just the good questions but probing ones as well. They are not meant to offend but offered for the entrepreneur not to be blindsided. They must not however be directly involved in the business not have any vested interest in it. They are simply friends on the lookout for what is best for a friend who sticks closer than a brother. They are not fair weather friends but stick with through the thick and thin. They are equally supportive in times of abundance and times of challenges when needed for encouragement or material things. They are not quick to draw with words but gun shy with finances. They are equally ready for any circumstance to come to the aid and succor of a friend.

Enterprising Employees

1 Kings 7:14 Expanded Bible (EXB)

14 ·Huram's mother was [He was the son of] a widow from the tribe of Naphtali. His father was from Tyre and had been ·skilled in making things from [a craftsman/artisan in] bronze. ·Huram [He] was also very skilled and ·experienced [knowledgeable; wise] in bronze work. So he came to King Solomon and did all ·the bronze [his] work.

Employees are to be treated as family members. They are genuinely appreciated and unconditionally accepted as beloved. They are to be trained slowly but corrected quickly. It must never be the reverse. They should not be released into responsibilities immediately and then not as swiftly pointed out when in error. Their attitude is ranked higher than their abilities. It is character that draw success not mere expertise. The virtues of the employee far out value his mastery of the job. The employee must not just be submissive to the work ethic of the entrepreneur. He must be comfortable with the company culture. He must not strive against it; but thrive along with the others. Strife does hinder the anointing of God in the workplace. Excellent employer-employee relations without reservation provide the true foundation for all the success hoped for in the marketplace. A company is only as acceptable to the consumers when it is perceived the workers are enjoying providing the services or producing the products.

Ephesians 6:9 J.B. Phillips New Testament (PHILLIPS)

[9] And as for you employers, be as conscientious and responsible towards those who serve you as you expect them to be towards you, neither misusing the power over others that has been put in your hands, nor forgetting that you are responsible yourselves to a heavenly employer who makes no distinction between master and man.

The golden rule is as applicable in the workplace as in any other venue. And it is not – he who has the gold, rules. It is act towards everyone as you would desire them to act towards you.

Concerned Customers

Ecclesiastes 7:5 Amplified Bible (AMP)
It is better to listen to the rebuke of the wise
man *and* pursue wisdom

Chapter Four: God's Entrepreneurial Keys

Than for one to listen to the song of fools *and* pursue stupidity.

Isolation from the marketplace is the worst idea ever. It is always beneficial to get out and get feedback from those served and those patronizing the products. Paid product endorsers are not any help at all. They are professionals ready to act out what is asked for by the script; they are not really satisfied customers. Product endorsers can be perceived as fakes just trying to entice viewers and listeners to make do with an inferior product when something out there is better. Word of mouth is far more superior to outdoor advertising and adds no extra costs. Comments and feedback are invaluable assets. It does not determine radical change but is open to adjustments for improvements. The entrepreneur must be wary of being enslaved by consumer power; he is not to please everyone just those that would really enjoy the merchandise and patronize the company faithfully through years to come passing on to the next generations the value of the service. Isn't that what God intended in the psalmist's voice of declaring His goodness from one generation to the next

– His mercies endureth forever? Catering to the needs not the whims of the customer is sound business practice. Keeping an open mind and a listening ear aids in bringing more worth to what the consumer gets in what is paid for. There is no substitute for a firm base of loyal customers that the entrepreneur endeavors to keep for several lifetimes after.

Viable Vendors

2 Kings 4:6-7 Good News Translation (GNT)

⁶ When they had filled all the jars, she asked if there were any more. "That was the last one," one of her sons answered. And the olive oil stopped flowing. ⁷ She went back to Elisha, the prophet, who said to her, "Sell the olive oil and pay all your debts, and there will be enough money left over for you and your sons to live on."

The vendors are the first face of the company as the ushers are in the church. Welcome is essential; vendors are crucial. They are not to be coming across as just wanting the customer to part with their cash; this trait is for shenanigans and con artists. Fraud is not the entrepreneur's hallmark; the vendors must possess not an iota of this malice. God the Entrepreneur reflected and represented in Christ; the vendor, likewise, is representation and reflection of the entrepreneur. They are to be developed into this mold. They are not to be taken for granted. They are primed in getting new customers. Of course, they are remunerated substantially and on time.

Accurate Accounting

Proverbs 27:23-24 Living Bible (TLB)

23-24 Riches can disappear fast. And the king's crown doesn't stay in his family forever—so watch your business interests closely. Know the state of your flocks and your herds;

Accounting of everything – inventory, merchandise, cash – is vital. A misguided concept and disorderly upkeep is ruinous. Profit margins, break-even points, fixed and variable expenses must be clearly delineated and examined to produce good decisions and proper adjustments. The main reference point should always be increase income, decrease costs. There must be a review of cash flow on a daily and weekly basis faithfully reported as recorded monthly and annually. Accounting records are a barometer of pricing and a parameter on debt financing.

Conscientious Contracts

Luke 12:57-59 The Message (MSG)

57-59 "You don't have to be a genius to understand these things. Just use your common sense, the kind you'd use if, while being taken to court, you decided to settle up with your accuser on the way, knowing that if the case went to the judge you'd probably go to jail and pay every last penny of the fine. That's the kind of decision I'm asking you to make."

All agreements must be documented; a whole page can already be utilized to put it all the salient points without the ubiquitous and secretive fine print. Disagreements over interpretation must be settled quickly. Misunderstandings can be avoided at the onset by clarifying terms at the beginning before signing. Court expenses are to be avoided at all costs. The time and expense are not worth bickering over. When possible, talks are to be done exhausting all possibilities rather than ending up before the magistrate. Prayer helps plentifully.

Complementary Competition

2 Samuel 7:1-2 Expanded Bible (EXB)

King David was living in his palace [house], and the Lord had given him peace [rest] from all his enemies around [sur-rounding] him [Deut. 12:10; apparently a sign that the conquest of Canaan was complete and the Temple should be built]. 2 Then David said to Nathan the prophet, "Look, I am living in a palace [house] made of cedar wood, but the Ark of God is[stays; dwells] in a tent!"

Competition need not be unfair. It is not a warfare. Competitors can and should live in peace with each other. Camaraderie and congeniality with the competition develops the entrepreneur into a better business leader of the community. Competitors become useful through prodding one to greater and more excellence in the friendly competition to offer the best. This redounds to greater and more satisfaction to the general public not just the consumers. Destructive competition of name-calling and down-grading distracts from the real issue of product excellence and unequalled service. The best product has yet to be manufactured; all services still need ample room for improvement. Friendliness, not enmity among competitors, guarantee pressing towards achieving this goal; it is to be prudently practiced.

Preferred Profits

Proverbs 11:25 Expanded Bible (EXB)

25 Whoever ·gives to others will get richer [or blesses others will be refreshed];

those who ·help [satisfy] others will themselves be ·helped [satisfied].

Proverbs 22:9 Expanded Bible (EXB)

9 Generous people ·will be blessed [or he will bless], because they share their food with the poor.

Companies give back to the community that caters to them. It must never be that the company simply enriches itself with the consumers in the community without giving back in terms of benefits for all (including those not patronizing their products) to enjoy. Generosity attracts generosity; giving begets giving. Each in turn, the community blesses the company; the company shares its success with the community. Donations, contributions, scholarships, disaster responses are affirmative actions projecting the concern of the company for the community's welfare. Pulling up stakes at the first sign of trouble forebodes ill for the company wherever it relocates. Caring and generous giving may even attract detractors to become potential customers.

Learning Leaders

Proverbs 19:20 New International Reader's Version (NIRV)

[20] Listen to advice and accept correction.
In the end you will be counted among those who are wise.

A community is not without business leaders. The entrepreneur must put premium value to the input of these leaders especially the ones that pioneered but not despising the up and coming new generation. A chamber of commerce or even a small group involvement goes a long way for the company to reap success among peers. The group is designed for learning among selves and accountability of character in handling the business. There is no end to learning. It continues until it can be sustained. The group is also the best venue to tutor the next business leaders of the future.

1 Timothy 2:1-3 The Message (MSG)

2 [1-3] The first thing I want you to do is pray. Pray every way you know how, for everyone you know. Pray especially for rulers and their governments to rule well so we can be quietly about our business of living simply, in humble contemplation. This is the way our Savior God wants us to live.

Chapter Five: Entrepreneurial Breakthrough

Everybody has to start somewhere. Everything must have a starting point. Only God does not have a beginning or an end. God is the Alpha (Beginning) and Omega (End).

If following through for generating income as an entrepreneur has not yet been started; it's time to act. Even the Bible advises against just hearing without doing.

James 1:21-25 Amplified Bible (AMP)

21 So get rid of all uncleanness and lall that remains of wickedness, and with a humble spirit receive the word [of God] which is implanted [actually rooted in your heart], which is able to save your souls. 22 But prove yourselves doers of the word [actively and continually obeying God's precepts], and not merely listeners [who hear the word but fail to internalize its meaning], deluding yourselves [by unsound reasoning contrary to the truth]. 23 For if anyone only listens to the word without obeying it, he is like a man who looks very

carefully at his natural face in a mirror; [24] for *once* he has looked at himself and gone away, he immediately forgets what he looked like. [25] But he who looks carefully into the perfect law, the *law* of liberty, and faithfully abides by it, not having become a [careless] listener who forgets but an active doer [who obeys], he will be blessed *and* favored by God in what he does [in his life of obedience].

The process of creating new income streams is different for everyone, so it is absolutely necessary not to want to model the approach exactly because knowledge, skills, and resources may not align with somebody else. Even so, it is understandable to at least learn something or the other from this chapter of entrepreneurial breakthrough.

Pray for an Idea

The very first step should be to pray for the idea. This should be obvious to all. God is the Entrepreneur; He is the one with the brilliant ideas. It is certainly not a bad idea to ask from Him His idea perfectly for the human entrepreneur.

The simplest ways is to grab your Bible with a pen and paper, and start reading listing down everything that catches attention. From the verses and the ideas or instructions, brainstorm the ideas for entrepreneurship among the other ideas like worship, virtues, values and actions. Among the entrepreneurship ideas, pick one that seems workable. Please don't go overboard by claiming by faith the impossible as the one that God wants. It may be, but is it ready?

If more help is needed to generate ideas; read more, pray more or even include fasting.

Many people get caught up trying to pick an idea. If you get stuck here, you can't progress. So whatever you do, don't let yourself get stuck here. Make a decision no matter what. Decide to aspire for more. Decide that what you have is enough. Just, decide.

The best way to choose among many different options is self-knowledge. Which of the choices best describes the entrepreneur's personality? That should narrow down the choices to the barest minimum unless one is too varied as a multi-faceted personality. Even then the multi-tasking bent exposes an inclination that should be the most likely choice. Otherwise, do it the apostles' way.

This may not sound so high-tech; it even smells of Old Testament longevity spilled over to the New Testament practices also dated but can still be received as working even in this day and age of nano-technology. Still it is better off that standing still and getting stuck with ideas that need to take off and not stared at for oblivion. Getting into action reasonably after much prayer and fasting is preferable to wrangling hands over self-doubt and being hindered from moving forward by useless delays. Progress is in trying your hand in at least a project or two rather than waiting for the opportune time to launch the perfect one. The projects under one's belt add up towards moving forward to the big one ahead. Creative people supposedly advice to fail faster to succeed later. God would not whisper that; He would rather intimate to take baby steps towards bigger strides later on.

Picking an idea is infinitely better than whining and complaining about the utter lack of good ideas coming along. It is actually an insult to the All-Wise Creator to admit a derelict of ideas, even bad ones. What was the brain created for? Where does imagination fail? Can God's creature really shake head and shrug shoulders and turn hands upward accepting defeat just about coming up with an idea? That's preposterous considering the Omniscience of the Creator God. 'I don't know' is also veritably unacceptable attitude when queried for a single simple idea. That's not possible. Impossible is not even having one idea. Improbable is running out of ideas.

The plain truth is that good income-generating ideas are a dime a dozen. Coming up with ideas is the easy quick immediate part. Even getting stuck in an employee's desk cannot that swiftly quench the inborn nature of the Creator speaking into being the innumerable species of birds, fishes, insects, flying and creeping land animals. If being stuck in the corporate world far too long, that perhaps the miniscule creative impulses have been squashed to make a better slave and clock-watcher; if that's the case, then go ask a nearby child what can be done to make the world better for people to live, and listen intently to what an innocent yet untainted by greed and envy has to offer. It's almost hearing God apart from His word.

Process the Idea

Most Christians have no inkling of what prayer really is all about. Basically, they know it is communication with God. But where does this conversation lead? To some it eventually ends up with the Christian asking from 'Daddy' God something in the Name of the Lord Jesus Christ. Well and good, but does it stop there? What if God wanted to reveal more primarily about Himself, about what Jesus has done for us and about what the future holds?

John 16:12-15 The Voice (VOICE)

12 I have so much more to say, but you cannot absorb it right now. 13-15 The Spirit of truth will come and guide you in all truth. He will not speak His own words to you; He will speak what He hears, revealing to you the things to come and bringing glory to Me. The Spirit has unlimited access to Me, to all that I possess and know,

Chapter Five: Entrepreneurial Breakthrough

just as everything the Father has is Mine. That is the reason I am confident He will care for My own and reveal the path to you.

Prayer processes the plans of God on earth; mostly what is to come. Thus the path of entrepreneurship comes from the Spirit of God. Depending on the nature of the entrepreneurial idea, details have to be decided next. However, it must be indelibly imprinted that destiny is not to be decided on; it is to be discovered. Deciding on the details is simply uncovering what God has already prepared.

Once again, it calls for more brainstorming possibilities; then picking on a detail or something, and moving forward.

Don't get caught up in vacillating. Just decide. The decision won't be perfect, and it doesn't have to be. Just pick an idea that seems pretty good, and run with it. It gets better along the way of picking better ideas once a few projects have been completed and evaluated how they turned out.

The author of Ecclesiastes is the wise King Solomon who even his father considered too young to build God's temple. So, David prepared everything before Solomon ascended to the throne. Then, wisely Solomon grew into a wise king whose wisdom was known throughout the known world. The Queen of Sheba traversed across plains and promontories to hear of his wisdom.

This same wise Solomon authored the Book of Wisdom, Proverbs, and it is given to would-be entrepreneurs to read this Bible book of 31 chapters several times before embarking on any project. The words of God in this book cannot just give ideas but also wise advises on how to implement the ideas.

Fall in Love with God and His Idea

The next step is to fall in love with your idea, the will of God in the Word of God. Most Christians are quick to respond that they love God above all yet slow to follow His injunction to read His Bible. That's incongruence. The books of Proverbs and Psalms put it quite clearly: The reverential fear of the Lord is the beginning of wisdom. The worship of God entails embracing His words. It is downright rude to supposedly love someone and yet not pay attention to a word they say. And this not just applies to teen-agers but to entrepreneurs and God-Entrepreneur.

The error of most people is missing the forest for the trees. They worship the creation missing the Creator. They are nature lovers without love for the nature Maker. They rave for the blessings forgetting the One Who blesses. They boast of Christianity and totally miss out on the Christ. Similarly, would-be entrepreneurs get so enamored with the project they forget to look to the One Who is the Author of all things. Even ministers of the gospel look to the channels of blessings, the conduit of the cash flow and totally disregard the Source.

Psalm 68:19 Lexham English Bible (LEB)

[19] Blessed be the Lord. Daily he loads us *with benefits*, the God *of* our salvation. *Selah*

The mistake these people often make is they look to their ideas to give them confidence, as if an idea itself can provide that. In reality almost all ideas are going to feel fuzzy and uncertain at first. Confidence comes in the knowledge that it comes from God.

1 Timothy 6:17-19J.B. Phillips New Testament (PHILLIPS)

Have a word for the rich

17-19 Tell those who are rich in this present world not to be contemptuous of others, and not to rest the weight of their confidence on the transitory power of wealth but on the living God, who generously gives us everything for our enjoyment. Tell them to do good, to be rich in kindly actions, to be ready to give to others and to sympathize with those in distress. Their security should be invested in the life to come so that they may be sure of holding a share in the life which is permanent.

The relationship is to the God Who gave the brain to come up with the idea or in some cases God Himself gives the idea. The nurturing of this relationship largely depends on how one responds to God and the God-given ideas.

Where does your relationship with God exist? Not in your mind; it is in the eternal Spirit. Where does your relationship with an idea from God exist? It is deposited in your mind subject to the word of God in the spirit.

Thinking ill about God as relationship partner and succumbing to doubts about the future He holds in His hands hinders the free flow of beautiful interchange in the relationship. Being in love with God and falling in love more and more each day enhances the extent to where the relationship can reach. It is not the same with the idea. Loving God involves trusting Him to be giving the best idea. The idea is not to be loved; God Who gave the idea is to be loved. Israel was so engrossed with Judaism; they turned their backs on God. Israel even completely forgot that Judaism was just the platform for the appearance of the Christ, the Savior of the world. Christians today are also so infatuated with Christianity – the bestselling books, the worship team, the church growth, the special meetings that they lose connection with the Head, Christ. Honor God and the idea will be in its proper place.

The idea is never the source of inspiration and motivation. God was, is and will always be. The idea actually stagnates if it is not nurtured and watered and allowed to germinate to its full potential. Still, it is just an idea. God is God. It can even be a good idea but not God's idea. In that case it is destined to fail.

Nevertheless knowing the idea comes from God puts the necessary boost to the commitment to see it through. No trial, trouble or tribulation could deter the pursuing the idea to its pre-determined conclusion.

Paul and his missionary band of brothers were on a roll. Timothy was added to the team and they wanted to gain more ground for Christ and headed towards inland Asia. It was a good idea but not God's idea. Twice they were rebuffed in implementing their own ideas. Finally, God had to show Paul what He wanted in a vision. There was a reason for that. So, they heeded God's instructions and headed for Europe. First stop, there was no synagogue. So, after scouting for a few days, they ended up in the river where fortuitously a wealthy woman merchant got converted. The next event wasn't so encouraging. Paul and Silas found themselves in the innermost dungeon under the earth. This is where the vision proves opportune. Had Paul not received the vision this incarceration can be misconstrued that crossing over to Macedonia was a bad idea? It was God's idea and Paul knew it and pursued it to the hilt. Success followed.

Make the Idea Work to produce what it was culled for

God's ideas always have purpose as in God's words. They accomplish what has been spoken. God's ideas will produce the desired result.

Isaiah 55:10-12 Amplified Bible, Classic Edition (AMPC)

10 For as the rain and snow come down from the heavens, and return not there again, but water the earth and make it bring forth and sprout, that it may give seed to the sower and bread to the eater,

11 So shall My word be that goes forth out of My mouth: it shall not return to Me void [without producing any effect, useless], but it shall accomplish that which I please *and* purpose, and it shall prosper in the thing for which I sent it.

12 For you shall go out [from the spiritual exile caused by sin and evil into the homeland] with joy and be led forth [by your Leader, the Lord Himself, and His word] with peace; the mountains and the hills shall break forth before you into singing, and all the trees of the field shall clap their hands.

Success is not an option. It is mandatory. It is also required to keep checking with headquarters ever so often for fresh instructions and updated details. Forgetting this important facet will cause a fumbling of the ball and dropping the project altogether.

Worldly entrepreneurs create and release products they clearly don't care much for. They'll usually spread the word for a few weeks, and then they give up and let the income stream die. People can tell it's an imitation, me-too product, jumping on the bandwagon, riding with the fad so they don't buy. With an also-ran product, this is enough discouragement to call it quits. With a product really coming out of the heart, however, even carnal entrepreneurs push through and keep putting the word out. How much more the Spirit-led Christian entrepreneur running with God's vision and idea?

Success is not an option; it is as sure as God is God.

But it's not enough to just create a cool product and hope people will buy it. People must be informed. It is incumbent to let people know about it. Once enough momentum is built, sales become self-sustaining, although it is presumptuous to assume this will happen automatically just because a product has been made and put on the Internet.

Some marketing vehicles that can be used are website and newsletter. Twitter and Google+ accounts can also be utilized to get the word out. Blogging about the development of this product along the way can also be seen as a way of marketing it. Many people who are following this entrepreneur book won't care about any product, but some will. So there will probably be some decent interest in the product when it launches. Expect to spend at least as much time marketing the new product or service as making it work. The amount of work in producing the product will also be the amount of labor getting the word. That's not so bad as it sounds. The Gospel took years to be formulated; it also took years to be proclaimed.

But the time will definitely arrive. The time to unveil the product, the time to usher in the profit has come.

Simplify a Completion Plan

A completion plan is what is to be done for the idea to be accomplished.

The previous steps in this article are pretty straightforward and can be done in less than a day of prayer and fasting (especially fasting – one day should be enough, three days is really, really being serious about it). If it takes longer than that, it's probably getting stuck in vacillating. Just make a decision at each step and move on.

Lots of interesting ideas die somewhere between the initial prayer for wisdom for the idea and full completion; pay closer attention to how to complete this and get it over and done with.

For single person projects, it doesn't make sense to get bogged down in over planning. Some people spend more time planning a project and getting ready to begin, when it would have taken less time to just dive in and do it as swiftly as possible. ASAP is helpful.

For larger projects involving more money, materials, manpower and machinery, care must especially be taken before any undertaking. No diving into deep waters without scuba gear.

To generate entrepreneur income, there is a way needed to maintain income without having to do so much grunt work to keep it going. To keep working each day to avoid seeing income drop, then it's earning active income, not entrepreneur income. It's the same as being employed. Entrepreneur income continues to flow even when the entrepreneur isn't actively working.

Many forms of entrepreneur income still require daily or weekly maintenance activities, such as fulfilling orders or handling customer service, but this doesn't mean performing those maintenance tasks by self. There must be delegating such tasks to other people, to businesses, or to technology. Income to be adjudged as really entrepreneur (meaning not having to do much to maintain cash flow), some items need to be removed from the plate, but those items still need to get done.

Entrepreneurship is an exercise in delegation. What is being delegated, and to whom? How will the necessary active tasks being handled if not done by self? Entrepreneurship provide these answers. Jesus the Entrepreneur delegated evangelism to the disciples.

Jesus delegated to His disciples the task of carrying the product (Gospel) to all the parts of the globe. That's globalization entrepreneurship. But this cannot work by a single proprietor; entrepreneurship entails delegation. Delegating to technology is a breeze because it is fast, efficient, consistent, and inexpensive. Technology also tends to scale well, meaning that one can add more computing resources, which generally requires little more than paying for those resources. This works well for an Internet business. It would be a massive effort if this had to be performed by human hands.

Notice then that when one relies on technology to communicate, one is already taking advantage of entrepreneur systems. Messages pass through equipment that's designed, built, and maintained by others. One may not be paying those people directly, but they're working every day. It's already taking advantage of these systems now. So if one currently relies on such systems for communication needs, then why not leverage them to handle income as well?

One can also delegate tasks to other people and to businesses to get them off the plate. In a typical affiliate deal, one may delegate the order processing, fulfillment, and customer service to another company. For example, use Amazon's affiliate program to sell items, effectively delegating a significant portion of the work to Amazon. From proper perspective an affiliate sale may seem very passive, but that's because Amazon provides the active labor to make affiliate commissions possible.

Invent or Improve

To employ own entrepreneur income system, there are several options:

1. Design and build own entrepreneur income system from scratch.
2. Learn how other people earn entrepreneur income and try to copy their approach.
3. Use someone else's system as-is (usually by paying for the privilege).
4. Do a combination of any of the above.

The most intelligent choice depends on a variety of factors including time constraints, budget constraints, personal strengths, and personal goals.

Those up for a real challenge, it can be very rewarding to design and implement own entrepreneur income system from scratch. The upside to this approach is that since one invented it, the one knows its inner workings, and can customize it all as wanted. The downside is that this method can take a lot of work, and it may be quite a while before the first income streams start flowing. Innovation is risky. Sometimes the risk pays off. Sometimes it doesn't.

More commonly, people borrow ideas from each other. Why reinvent the wheel? Learn what works for other people, and use similar methods. There are plenty of books and systems authored by entrepreneurs who are happy to teach how to do what they did. Some people are willing to share details of their systems for free, while others only share this info for a fee. Even when there is a fee, buying someone else's system can save a tremendous amount of time and energy.

A seemingly inexpensive approach is to use someone else's system as-is. An example of this is licensing a book to a book publisher or selling the book via Amazon. This may seem like a good deal since the author does not have to pay anything up front, but it can be a lot more expensive if the book does well because one may have to give away a significant percentage of sales to the system provider. This approach tends to be the easiest for getting started. System providers in this category may be very good at processing orders and handling customer service, but they usually don't provide much marketing assistance, so it may be hard to get noticed with them. That said, they can do an awful lot of work making income streams very passive.

There is the hybrid approach of combining methods. It entails that one picks up many good ideas from others, then put own spin on things and keep tweaking passive income streams.

Purchasing or Producing

Is purchasing someone else's brainchild better for setting up an entrepreneurship or is producing one more beneficial in the long run? Buying into someone else's system, such as by paying for their knowledge or resources, is the shortcut that may lead to a dead-end. Producing one's own is the longer route that may be abandoned due to tediousness.

Generally this is a good idea, especially when one's first starting out, but only if one is extremely cautious about it. One can waste a lot of money buying low quality money-making systems from random Internet marketers. On the other hand, paying for a good system can also deliver tremendous value. One can learn in a short period of time what took someone else years or even decades of painstaking work to piece together.

One must not be too over-eager in paying for what seemed like premium knowledge in this area, and waste money on what turned out to be fluffy or outdated info. The offshoot is to cut back massively and become very stingy which may cause one to miss some easy opportunities. The more practical and realistic attitude is to be willing to pay for systems know-how if it can be applied effectively and if the info comes from a quality source. A quality source is someone who seems to genuinely want to help people understand and apply the methods they teach, rather than just selling low-quality info to make more money. Also, a quality system is one that's already been proven to work under real-world conditions.

Usually when one pays for systems knowledge these days, one is not looking to implement someone else's system as-is, simply looking for a few fresh ideas for use to upgrade existing systems. What are the latest and greatest ideas one might otherwise miss?

When it comes to marketing, the people who sell these systems may try to push emotional buttons and offer extra incentives to get one to buy. It is best to ignore those sales tactics and look at the potential value more objectively.

Entrepreneur Income System Inclination

Does one want an income-generating website? Is one leaning towards having a product to sell on other people's websites? Would one like a system that incorporates both? Or does one want to do something incredibly totally wildly different?

Think about strengths for a moment. A good system will allow one to leverage strengths while delegating the areas of weakness. Is one a content machine where one needs a system to provide an effective publishing platform and a way to monetize work? Would one feel more comfortable selling someone else's product or service? Does selling turn one off, and would one prefer to delegate the selling aspect as well?

When it comes to entrepreneur income systems, the key test is whether the system works in the real world. One can dream up whatever one likes, but dreams aren't streams.

A good entrepreneur income system generates results. If one has never created own system from scratch, it is highly recommended that borrowing someone else's system to reach goal quickly. Otherwise if one prefers a bigger challenge and don't mind investing a lot more of time and energy up front, it's all too easy and always free to roll one's own.

Once one has had the experience of working with someone else's system, one may decide to keep using it, experiment with different systems, or tackle the challenge of rolling own system. There's no right or wrong way to do it. It is however strongly suggested that for the first stream of entrepreneur income, it's much easier to simply borrow and apply someone else's system, even if it has to be paid for. A good system looks simple, but that's because it hides so many implementation details. For entrepreneur income, this is a good thing. Handling too many details throws back into the realm of employment income.

A good entrepreneur income system will normally employ many different income-generating strategies simultaneously, weaving them into a congruent tapestry. This is similar to how a computer integrates many different hardware and software components that function well as a unit..

Loving God's Ordained System

At this point it is too early to commit to a particular entrepreneur income system approach. Eventually it will be needed to make such a commitment, but for the moment familiarizing with some options and giving this some thought is a good enough start.

Which aspects of entrepreneur income systems appear best? Do they play to one's strengths? Are they expected to work if utilized? How might one adapt and extend them?

It's important to cultivate a healthy respect with the entrepreneur income system. The system liked will be likely used; the system despised will be laid at the wayside.

Real estate investing is a possible entrepreneurial generating income for those who are inclined to it and not be bored to tears; it must be something worthwhile and counted as contributing much. Some people may be very passionate about real estate investing, but it must not be bad fit for the entrepreneur's personality and values.

On the other hand, blogging can also be an entrepreneurial generating income. Try other ideas so as not to make the mistake of adopting an entrepreneur income system that one merely tolerates. The system must be truly appreciated. Offload the work that is not enjoyable. Doing what one enjoys contributes more and is better for everyone concerned and benefitted.

Keep Life Simple

God simplifies life; the devil complicates. It's easy to bite off more than can be chewed with the first passive income idea. A track record of successfully completing large projects can no longer be stopped. But if one has a tendency to get discouraged and give up too soon, it is suggested scaling down the ambitions. Build confidence through smaller projects to others that can actually be completed.

It's better to complete a 30-page eBook and sell it for $7 and generate a few sales per month than it is to tackle a 200-page writing project and never get it done. The former provides some genuine value to people; the latter will merely frustrate the entrepreneur.

Treat earlier projects as training for developing success muscles. The greatest predictor of future success is actually past success, so think about creating some simple successes by taking on modest projects and getting them done and released. Once done with a few of those, then consider scaling up and tackling bigger projects. Even with seemingly simple projects, one is going to learn a lot. The entrepreneur gets faster, and then it will be easier to scale up and tackle larger projects.

It's so easy to underestimate how long things will take by overlooking details. If one has never created an entrepreneur income stream before, the first project may involve lots of one-time steps like setting up an online shopping cart. But again once done with that initial setup work, similar streams with greater ease simply be made by plugging them into the same system.

Try not to get overly excited about making a killing with the first entrepreneur income project. Place attention on learning the ropes and generate a nice little stream. Then one can scale up by creating more streams. If one can generate even $50 a month with the first stream, it's off to a good start. It's generally harder to go from $0 to $50 a month than it is to go from $50 to $500 per month.

Reality vs. Research

There are two main schools of thought on how to pick income-producing creative projects. One is to go with your gut and do whatever inspires you. If you get an idea for a new project, run with it right away. The other idea is to research what people actually want to buy and then create something for that target market. This is the classic "find a need and fill it approach."

The best results can be gained by combining both approaches. First, be saturated in trying to understand what people need (This is God's heart first and foremost!).

Luke 10:2 Amplified Bible (AMP)

2 He was saying to them, "The harvest is abundant [for there are many who need to hear the good news about salvation], but the workers [those available to proclaim the message of salvation] are few. Therefore,[prayerfully] ask the Lord of the harvest to send out workers into His harvest.

God knows what His creation needs. God knows what man needs. Therefore, it is incumbent for the entrepreneur to be thinking like God in seeking to provide what the people need. The entrepreneurs are few and in between while the needs grow larger day after day.

Just as the Holy Spirit knows the needs of believers to be raised in prayer; the entrepreneur through the Holy

Spirit can know the needs of the people and pray to God to give him the necessary tools to meet those needs to generate income.

Other than this, online research, surveys, or just talking to people can also work.. Over the years hundreds of people met helps one better understand their needs and what can be provided that will be helpful to them. More so to someone always praying to God to meet these people's needs; God will reveal to this praying entrepreneur what is needed.

Ephesians 4:28-29 Amplified Bible (AMP)

[28] The thief [who has become a believer] must no longer steal, but instead he must work hard [making an honest living], producing that which is good with his own hands, so that he will have *something* to share with those in need.[29] Do not let unwholesome [foul, profane, worthless, vulgar] words ever come out of your mouth, but only such *speech* as is good for building up others, according to the need *and* the occasion, so that it will be a blessing to those who hear [you speak].

Entrepreneurship is all about meeting needs. Meeting needs is all about finding out what is needed. The entrepreneur becomes a blessing from God meeting the need and not just another person raking in an income.

The church is already an existing audience for market research, that's a great place to start, but one can easily gather information from other sources. This type of mental saturation is a good place to begin because it helps narrow focus, so generating ideas would not turn out to be an overwhelming task. After that the entrepreneur can start brainstorming some potential design ideas. Taking in a lot of input really helps when it comes to generating ideas. In going through this possibly tedious by necessary process, the entrepreneur won't help but notice gaps in other people's creations that helps the entrepreneurs see where to take things in a different direction, thereby contributing something unique.

Once an idea (through much praying and asking around and tinkering about) becomes inspired (further by the Holy Spirit), it will still take a lot of work to implement. The power of market research is accurately finding out what the people need and create a product that they would actually purchase to make the entrepreneur do a lot better financially.

Market Research Pertinent Actions

The actual market research must not be much ado about nothing. There are so many variables that one can get bogged down in analysis paralysis if overdoing all the inputs of all the data of all the research. Take a pretty light-weight approach to market research. Less is best. Again (with God's help) mainly look for two things:

1. What do people already have but still need?
2. Where are there gaps with relatively high demand and low supply that one could potentially serve?

Sometimes it's hard to answer #1 directly because probably there is really no access to other people's sales figures. But one can often use other public data to make some educated guesses. Of course, there is trending and there is pioneering. Although an entrepreneur is innately a pioneer, he must also have keen insight in what is trending as emerging need. The genius is not just in being the frontrunner but a wise guy who jumps in past the proverbial first angst over unaccepted value but before the onslaught of saturation point. Somewhere before the middling is just about right timing. Then if it is not destined as long haul but temporary assignment, there is now the even more astute timing of getting off before getting burned. Rankings of products and services are also a great help. Products can be so overdeveloped that they stagnate in a plateau of being ranked in the top 10 for the last millennia. It is not going anywhere but down in the second millennium. Other products can be so rapidly developing that the there is an annual discard resulting in a glut of the product proving it unsalable at a certain level. Even popularity is a healthy gauge as far as it can be carried. What is popular for a period turns into antique right in the most recent successive period! All this information helps the entrepreneur make an educated guess (apart from the promptings of the Holy Spirit) which direction to take to meet the most marketable needs of the consumers. Thus, it is easy to see how to serve the people in their needs and make money through doing so.

Without help from above, it can be a tricky balancing act between making something that inspires and making something that people need and both must be sellable. There's surely some luck and randomness involved too unless one is really a believer of God and His word. But in the world's system of consumerism situations show where results are 10, 20, or 50 times better when creators finally agree to give customers what they need instead of trying to convince customers to want what's been created.

Should there be an ultimate sacrifice of artistic integrity to satisfy the public? No, it's not necessary to do that. Should there be a giving up of spiritual identity as an entrepreneur and a believer? Definitely, no one should reach this point of crisis. People who feel they must choose one or the other are creating a false dichotomy due to limiting beliefs and blocks to making good money as God intended. No one should feel pressured to give up beliefs and integrity just to gain a buck. Paying more attention to what other people needs makes one a better entrepreneur; more customers should appreciate new creations suited for the need not just for the income. Can you take the pulse of what other people need to buy and then focus on pursuing inspired ideas that will land somewhere in the general vicinity? That's wisdom.

James 1:5-8 Amplified Bible (AMP)

5 If any of you lacks wisdom [to guide him through a decision or circumstance], he is to ask of [our benevolent] God, who gives to everyone generously and without rebuke *or* blame, and it will be given to him. 6 But he must ask [for wisdom] in faith, without doubting [God's willingness to help], for the one who doubts is like a billowing surge of the sea that is blown about and tossed by the wind. 7 For such a person ought not to think *or* expect that he will receive anything [at all] from the Lord, 8 *being* a double-minded man, unstable *and* restless in all his ways [in everything he thinks, feels, or decides].

Much of the time when artists claim to be undiscovered geniuses and lament that they can't make money doing what they love, the more likely truth is that their art just isn't very good yet. The deeper truth is that they refuse to acknowledge God as the Source of all wisdom. Entrepreneurs, like artists, must see the need from God's perspective of what is best for mankind and then proceed to make money out of providing for this need which God intended in the first place.

James 1:17-18 Amplified Bible (AMP)

[17] Every good thing given and every perfect gift is from above; it comes down from the Father of lights [the Creator and Sustainer of the heavens], in whom there is no variation [no rising or setting] or shadow cast by His turning [for He is perfect and never changes]. [18] It was of His own will that He gave us birth [as His children] by the word of truth, so that we would be a kind of first fruits of His creatures [a prime example of what He created to be set apart to Himself — sanctified, made holy for His divine purposes].

Some of the best art is developed with a strong social component, meaning that there's ongoing feedback between the artist and the patrons. Similarly the best entrepreneur endeavors are those coming from God inspiring the believer and resulting in providing for the needs of the people thereby generating income for the entrepreneur.

Reasonable Trade-offs not Belief Compromises

The distinct advantage of knowing what people need is being so very sure of that point when one is bordering in going against these needs to some extent and making this choice consciously with deluding self.

Sometimes (but it should be more often) the entrepreneur could predict in advance that income could be greater doing a certain project over another. Yet, despite this grave prognosis, an entrepreneur God's way would follow the Spirit's leading to pursue an inspiring project with lower income just for the joy of it. The success felt can catapult the entrepreneur to greater heights having been set free into prostituting self for the god mammon rather than just doing what is inspiring and uplifting. God honors such virtue and rewards with wisdom for other projects that would certainly generate greater wealth.

So in this case, the research gave an idea of what to expect. The action done after the decision based on the information (plus revelation) gathered cannot be counted as a disappointment since it was already known beforehand the low turn-out of cash. It was done anyway from the heart not from the cash register.

It's nice (infinitely better actually) to get an idea of what the trade-offs are when putting other concerns ahead of making money. Then it becomes very easy to crow about the freedom to create what God decided as the people's need as worth the financial impact. There's no right or wrong way to make these decisions. It's a matter of personal preference. The thrill is in making different choices over time and seeing how each type of project plays out – one for money, one for prestige and one for the sheer joy of it but ultimately all for the glory of God.

Making Risks work

Faith works. From man's viewpoint, faith is a leap taking too many chances. From God's view, faith is taking Him at His word without any risks involve. A person in a burning building may risk jumping hearing voices shouting below – "Jump a net is waiting!"; even though failing to see the alleged catcher through the thick black smoke. Yet, a familiar voice of someone whom the man in the ledge trusts is no risk at all. The net will be there to catch him because a trustworthy voice said so!

With new and untested ideas, there's always some risk involved, but everyone has a different levels of risk tolerance. Godly entrepreneurs more likely will go by their level of faith.

An entrepreneur of the baby talk or infant type of faith should fall back more on reliable market research in order to do a better job of what people need and the corresponding product to produce. That way time is not wasted on making and merchandising a product that will be a flop. Faith knows no such limits. Believing the project   is from God gives the entrepreneur the confidence to put foot forward and deliver on a product that will be well received.

The more faithful entrepreneur (or risk taker as the world defines such an individual) will take calculated changes due to inner promptings of the Spirit taking the chance of embarking in something completely novel with or without the benefit of a market research. Success from another's worldview is far from guaranteed, but it is not stumbling in the dark upon some previously unknown need that becomes in demand. Fate is not faith.

This is a matter of personal confidence in God through faith and preferences may change depending on what else is going on in one's life. It's like any form of investing. Is it wiser to want to play it safe and deal with relatively predictable outcomes, or is it bolder to want to take a chance and explore uncharted territory? Ask God. He has all the answers. He is always right.

Ultimately all the earthly tools can be bypassed and the entrepreneur can just run with whatever inspiration received from the Holy Spirit once clearly established. Otherwise, the more prudent way is to take small steps towards that direction watching out for warnings from the Spirit when to stand still and when to proceed pretty much like the leading of the Israelites in the wilderness from Egypt to the Promised Land.

A barometer of faith used by adherents is excitement. This can also be perceived as the leading of the Spirit. When the excitement is high, one is prone to surmise (rightly so according to faith proponents) that the leading is strong and the project should proceed rapidly.

When the excitement dwindles, it is construed as warning bells to slow down for opposition may just be around the corner waiting to trip up the entrepreneur. When the excitement wanes, it's time to fold up the project. It is always exciting to try something new but caution must be exercised to be able to handle the downside should the project not perform as expected. This is quite workable for small entrepreneur projects not demanding so much time, effort and resources. The setback is a learning experience not too grievous to discourage the entrepreneur to quit.

An entrepreneur with enough successful projects can afford to take more chances in venturing to other entrepreneurial projects. An entrepreneur just starting out should be more circumvent regarding tackling projects. At any rate, a conservative entrepreneur will make sure the projects tackled meet needs and therefore have sure strong demand.

A lot of this research can be done with free tools and public information. For example, one can see how well any book is selling relative to any other book by checking the sales rankings on Amazon.com. For all kinds of products now, the entrepreneur can get a decent idea of how well any particular product is selling just by looking at public data. This is not difficult even with a modicum of decent Internet skills.

Inspiration Always

Oftentimes as it is wont, an entrepreneur God's way receives inspired ideas before any market research is done concerning the project. This is the norm not the exemption. It is the same with pastors reading the text first and receiving revelation before checking out the commentaries. In the entrepreneur's case the market research is and after the fact afterthought to validate or to wait on the idea more. Rumination is paramount in this case as in a cook making the stew simmer longer while savoring the smell. The entrepreneur meditates (gets the idea rolling in his mind over and over again thinking out all the possibilities) longer. Prayer and fasting may also be resorted to before finally wading in the shallow waters first diving into deeper shoals later on.

There is another way of conducting an informal market research for a project. It is called social media. The proliferation of these conduits is to the entrepreneur's advantage. The idea is floated around for response from those afflicted by nanophobias who don't want to miss anything recent in the status. A thousand likes or comments may be pointing towards a favorable outcome for the project. There is however the risk of someone else stealing the idea and running away with the project. It would be then safer to bounce around the ideas with reliable friends that won't end up competitors. Otherwise, at any time and any location the idea can be broached to any one and the reaction adjudged to proceed or wait longer before launching the project.

There is still another way to conduct market research. Dive in and test the idea in the real world. Then the know-how actually develops in the doing. The benefit to this approach is that one might just stumble upon something that works really well. Then the entrepreneur can build an empire around it not forgetting that kingdom of God building is foremost.

The entrepreneur God's way is naturally right before God and keeps self right before God from the starting idea to the running with the vision through accomplishing the goal and finishing the race with aplomb all because of God and His grace (unmerited favor). There are no besetting fears of failing but calculated steps inspired by the Holy Spirit.

The entrepreneur God's way is more courageous than most people; courage can give serious uncompromising advantage because it cuts down on competition. One reason entrepreneurship pays so well is that so many people are afraid of it, so it's not as competitive as other fields. So if one is willing to go where others are afraid to go, most of would-be competitors will surrender those markets to the bold entrepreneur.

Courage is contagious. Note that after God's pep talk, Joshua immediately confers with the leaders and influenced them.

Joshua 1:16-18Living Bible (TLB)

16 To this they fully agreed and pledged themselves to obey Joshua as their commander-in-chief.

17-18 "We will obey you just as we obeyed Moses," they assured him, "and may the Lord your God be with you as he was with Moses. If anyone, no matter who, rebels against your commands, he shall die. So lead on with courage and strength!"

These are quite strong words. The entrepreneur's henchmen may not have to resort to murder but it is utterly comforting to have people around egging one to always be courageous, bold and resolute.

Courage must be well-placed since idea selection has a lot to do with risk tolerance. The less risk tolerant or little faith one has, the more the entrepreneur will want to rely on market research and assessing need and corresponding demand to guide the decisions. As faith a.k.a. risk tolerance in the world's parlance increases, the entrepreneur can afford to take on projects that rely more heavily on going with the flow of inspiration, but even in those cases, one may still choose to validate them with a little market research to gain enough confidence to get moving. In retrospect there is none more powerful than the word of God as guide.

Hebrews 4:11-13Amplified Bible (AMP)

11 Let us therefore make every effort to enter that rest [of God, to know and experience it for ourselves], so that no one will fall by *following* the same example of disobedience [as those who died in the wilderness]. 12 For the word of God is living and active *and* full of power [making it operative, energizing, and effective]. It is sharper than any two-edged sword, penetrating as far as the division of the soul and spirit [the completeness of a person], and of both joints and marrow [the deepest parts of our nature], exposing *and* judging the very thoughts and intentions of the heart.13 And not a creature exists that is concealed from His sight, but all things are open *and* exposed, and revealed to the eyes of Him with whom we have to give account.

Entrepreneurship God's way is entering into a rest of successful project not toiling and travailing for a few measly coins. That is never the way to traverse. The word of God clearly delineates which way to go. It also promises a reckoning of the resources given to be applied for good use. Every step is ordered and nothing is hid to the God Entrepreneur Who goes before the believer entrepreneur. The word points out in crystal clear manner the huge difference between a seemingly good idea and the error-free God idea. After all, God is the Prime Investor in the entrepreneurship beholden to the believer. It is to Him that the entrepreneur accounts the enterprise bestowed upon. Stewardship is accountability as much as responsibility. God has graced the entrepreneur with the ability to respond properly to inspired ideas, market research and the appropriate action needed to be undertaken.

It is a given that the entrepreneur is a born-again believer instructed in the ways of the Lord never deviating from it to the right or to the left but steadily moving forward keeping both eyes focused on the Lord Jesus Christ who leads the way by the Holy Spirit. Otherwise, the road becomes fraught with evils and dangers designed by the enemy to distract the entrepreneur from God's goals. This is the set purpose and plan of God for every entrepreneur and every establishing enterprise. There is no room for divine error but just human missteps easily correctible by heaven's headquarters from which all blessings flow.

Since the entrepreneur is partnering with God in going through all these creativity to share some valuable project people really need and not just want or demand, it is virtually incumbent to rely heavily on God's provision and guidance every step of the way. There is absolutely no room for second-guessing God or trying to impress God by inserting one's own ideas.

What if you can't come up with any ideas at all? Fast and pray. Shedding off all excess baggage crowding the brain and short circuiting the though process are quieted before the Presence of God. In the final analysis, what is to be accomplished is God's goal of transformation. Should this purpose of God be done through entrepreneurship, so be it! Along the way to transformation people's needs are met, products and services are created and marketed and income is generated to be plowed back to more enterprises and to the propagation of the Gospel. AMEN.

Chapter Six: Manifestations Don't Lie

Proverbs 22:13Amplified Bible (AMP)

13 The lazy one [manufactures excuses and] says,

"There is a lion outside!

I will be killed in the streets [if I go out to work]!"

These wisdom couplets are not for the entrepreneur. Although these verses point out to a sluggard; the secondary sense also applies to those who stays put and sit on their dreams. Someone once remarked that the graveyard is the place to visit if one wants to fellowship with unfulfilled dreams. Death does cut short any lofty ambitions or endless possibilities. It is then wise to hearken to a voice from the not-too-distant past – the admonitions of the pragmatic James.

James 4:13-17Amplified Bible (AMP)

13 Come now [and pay attention to this], you who say, "Today or tomorrow we will go to such and such a city, and spend a year there and carry on our business and make a profit." 14 Yet you do not know [the least thing] about what may happen in your life tomorrow. [What is

secure in your life?] You are *merely* a vapor [like a puff of smoke or a wisp of steam from a cooking pot] that is visible for a little while and then vanishes [into thin air].[15] Instead you ought to say, "If the Lord wills, we will live and we will do this or that." [16] But as it is, you boast [vainly] in your pretension *and* arrogance. All such boasting is evil. [17] So any person who knows what is right to do but does not do it, to him it is sin.

God's grand plan for humanity keeps moving forward with or without the consent of man. A writer compares the congruence of God's sovereignty and man's free will to an ocean liner crossing the Atlantic in a trans-ocean voyage from London to New York. The passengers can freely do anything their hearts desire while the behemoth steadily moves on towards the destination. Nothing the passengers do can deter the ship from reaching the opposite port. God's plans move forward and what the entrepreneur does with what God has given him will not halt the progress the purposes of God are manifesting.

Proverbs 16:1-2Expanded Bible (EXB)

Chapter Six: Manifestations Don't Lie

16 People may make plans in their minds [hearts], but only the Lord can make them come true [from the Lord comes a responding tongue].

² ·You may believe you are doing right [All paths of people are pure in their eyes],
but the Lord will judge your reasons [measure your motives; weigh the spirits].

When people fail to move forward in the direction of their dreams, a common excuse is "I don't know how." They claim that a lack of know-how is the key factor holding them back in life. An excuse is simply that and nothing else, an excuse that is absolutely lame and utterly useless. It amounts to nothing. It accomplishes nothing. It cannot even excuse self. It's a dead end without any hope of being revived. It is better off left alone and not even tried to be resuscitated.

People lament all the time saying that they wish they could start a successful career, but they just don't know how. They act as if magically they will be bestowed with some kind of insider knowledge that isn't equally accessible to all. The truth is that no one really knows how to do something new until they've done it. In fact it is God's law of learning.

This is sound sensible advice to serious entrepreneurs God's way. Any other path is inordinate and disoriented leading to unwarranted excess or to the other extreme of confused mess. Carefully and circumspectly, the entrepreneur weighs every option considering every opposition and accompanying possibility once overcame always praying and giving thanks every step of the way. This leads to success and averts disaster at every turn; but this is not the likely path taken by the whiners and complainers, scoffers and mockers so predominant in this day and age.

As it was with Moses in the wilderness ...

Numbers 11:1Amplified Bible (AMP)

11 Now the people became like those who complain *and* whine about their hardships, and the Lord heard it; and when the Lord heard it, His anger was kindled, and the fire of the Lord burned among them and devoured those in the outlying parts of the camp.

Chapter Six: Manifestations Don't Lie

So it was with Jesus in His ministry …

Luke 15:2Amplified Bible (AMP)

2 Both the Pharisees and the scribes *began* muttering *and* complaining, saying, "This man accepts *and* welcomes sinners and eats with them."

John 6:61Amplified Bible (AMP)

61 But Jesus, aware that His disciples were complaining about it, asked them, "Does this cause you to stumble *and* take offense?

So it was with the first church …

Acts 6:1Amplified Bible (AMP)

6 Now about this time, when the number of disciples was increasing, a complaint was made by the Hellenists (Greek-speaking Jews) against the [native] Hebrews, because their widows were being overlooked in the daily serving *of food.*

And continued on and on …

Jude 16Amplified Bible (AMP)

16 These *people* are [habitual] murmurers, griping *and* complaining, following after their own desires [controlled by passion]; they speak arrogantly,

[pretending admiration and] flattering people to *gain an* advantage.

Yet these complainers can be so easily swayed to change their tunes; all they are waiting for is a dole-out or a greater incentive to get off their backsides and get moving with the program. An offer of million-dollar-bribe to generate results at the shortest possible time and every excuse and pointless whining are solidly blasted out of the water. Somehow the lack of knowledge is no longer a serious obstacle for them.

With sufficient motivation, one can simply go out and acquire whatever knowledge is required. All the raw how-to information needed is probably available online for free anyway. Either that or one can figure out what is really needed via trial and error if one just starts taking action. And of course, there is God Who was, Who is and Who is to come. There is His word for instruction and correction. There is the Holy Spirit, the Helper and Strengthener. There is the Lord Jesus Christ, Savior and Redeemer. There is God and His promise.

There is no room for excuses in the entrepreneur's enterprise. Claiming lack of certain knowledge is an act of denying self permission to experience what is desired. It's a way of blocking self from moving toward goal which does not even belong to the entrepreneur but to God , the Author of the vision and mission.

The physical and mental act of acquiring knowledge is really a projection of a deeper event that occurs within the consciousness. That event is the act of giving self permission to progress to a new revelation to shift away from the current experience of reality and to graduate to a new experiential level.

Prayer cannot be undermined. These prayers can be personally prayed for by the entrepreneur for self and see a transformation from fawning to fiercely forceful. The strength comes from the inner being indwelt by the Mighty Holy Spirit hovering above the waters in Creation and then creating what was spoken to be. Light be and there was light!

When spiritual consciousness experiences that internal shift, all the knowledge need will practically show up at the doorstep as revelation from God. In many cases it's not even required to have new knowledge or new revelation, but if it is really needed and asked for, then it is experientially known and not just head knowledge experience, a learning phase in both the spiritual and physical reality as progressing to the next level.

Peter was introduced to the Christ at the onset of His ministry; he makes the confession three years later. The knowledge of Jesus as the Christ grew from information to revelation.

John 1:35-42 Amplified Bible (AMP)

Jesus' Public Ministry, First Converts

35 Again the next day John was standing with two of his disciples, 36 and he looked at Jesus as He walked along, and said, "Look! The Lamb of God!"37 The two disciples heard him say this, and they followed Jesus. 38 And Jesus turned and saw them following Him, and asked them, "What do you want?" They answered Him, "Rabbi (which translated means Teacher), where are You staying?" 39 He said to them, "Come, and you will see." So they went [with Him] and saw where He was staying; and they stayed with Him that day, for it was

about the tenth hour. [40] One of the two who heard what John said and [as a result] followed Jesus was Andrew, Simon Peter's brother. [41] He first looked for *and* found his own brother Simon and told him, "We have found the Messiah" (which translated means the Christ). [42] Andrew brought Simon to Jesus. Jesus looked at him and said, "You are Simon the son of John. You shall be called Cephas (which is translated Peter)."

Matthew 16:13-20Amplified Bible (AMP)

Peter's Confession of Christ

[13] Now when Jesus went into the region of Caesarea Philippi, He asked His disciples, "Who do people say that the Son of Man is?" [14] And they answered, "Some say John the Baptist; others, Elijah; and still others, Jeremiah, or [just] one of the prophets." [15] He said to them, "But who do you say that I am?" [16] Simon Peter replied, "You are the Christ (the Messiah, the Anointed), the Son of the living God." [17] Then Jesus answered him, "Blessed [happy, spiritually secure, favored by God] are you, Simon son of Jonah, because flesh and blood (mortal man) did not reveal this to you, but My

Chapter Six: Manifestations Don't Lie

Father who is in heaven. [18] And I say to you that you are Peter, and on this rock I will build My church; and the gates of Hades (death) will not overpower it [by preventing the resurrection of the Christ]. [19] I will give you the keys (authority) of the kingdom of heaven; and whatever you bind [forbid, declare to be improper and unlawful] on earth will have [already] been bound in heaven, and whatever you loose [permit, declare lawful] on earth will have[already] been loosed in heaven." [20] Then He gave the disciples strict orders to tell no one that He was the Christ (the Messiah, the Anointed).

Peter moved from the level of walking with Jesus as a disciple to being identified with Him as an apostle. There was visible leveling up.

Why would an entrepreneur ever want to block self from going up a level? Why would one stay stuck for so long with feeble excuses like "I don't know how" or "I don't know what to do"?

The unequivocal answer is that the entrepreneur is not ready yet to progress. All the lessons of physical reality have not been soaked up much less the spiritual reality.

Entrepreneurship is an earthly activity with eternal repercussions. A preacher likened it to filling up one's curriculum vitae for use in eternity. Everything done on earth as a believer (in this case, an entrepreneur) measures the extent of the believer's scope of reach forever. Missteps and mishaps (due to the inclination towards the 'perhaps') will cost the believer eternal rewards.

Every entrepreneur is prepared by God for a task. Paul as a minister had an anointing for that office. The believer who has been chosen for such has an equal anointing for the entrepreneurship. But as Paul advises, utmost care must be exercised in completing the task whether ministering or being an entrepreneur. There are no two ways about it. It is ordained by God. All that is required of the entrepreneur is to believe, trust God completely and act accordingly. All actions are based on the belief system forged by the word of God unto iron-clad shield of faith to thwart the evil darts of the enemy that may amount to doubts and disbelief. This may result in the entrepreneur being disqualified for the price of a bonanza of income here in this earth and crowns to come in heaven.

People who complain about not progressing are like video game players who complain that they can't pass the current level. But to pass the current level the enemy must be overcome, something must be done. Now if fear petrifies the entrepreneur unto a catatonic state of permanent coma then there is no next level to speak of. The game ends there. The entrepreneur's enterprise goes kaput. The end has come. Another preacher strongly contends that Christianity is not for wimps. Definitely, entrepreneurship is also not for the easily scared who can be effortless fodder for the roaring lion seeking who can be devoured.

I believe in prosperity just like I believe in holiness without which no man shall see the Lord. What I advocate for is a balance gospel that teaches these principles with their roots embedded in scriptures. Many prosperity preachers will admit to being stuck at the financial level of being broke constantly struggling against debt. They knew they couldn't get pass this financial bind without God's help. Thus, they resorted to resisting the enemy at this level claiming the blessings of Abraham as theirs being one with the Seed of Abraham. They took God for His word. They got out of Satan's game plan of accepting poverty as God's way of sanctifying believers removing from them carnality evident in their love of the things in this world. They hopped into God's way in the Kingdom.

They believed. They spoke. They received revelation from God how to prosper. The wealth and riches manifested. Manifestations don't lie.

Paul as both missionary and tent-maker has the same mindset an entrepreneur must have.

Philippians 4:10-14Amplified Bible (AMP)

God's Provisions

[10] I rejoiced greatly in the Lord, that now at last you have renewed your concern for me; indeed, you were concerned about me *before*, but you had no opportunity to show it. [11] Not that I speak from [any personal] need, for I have learned to be content [and self-sufficient through Christ, satisfied to the point where I am not disturbed or uneasy] regardless of my circumstances. [12] I

know how to get along and live humbly [in difficult times], and I also know how to enjoy abundance *and* live in prosperity. In any and every circumstance I have learned the secret [of facing life], whether well-fed or going hungry, whether having an abundance or being in need. [13] I can do all things [which He has called me to do] through Him who strengthens *and* empowers me [to fulfill His purpose—I am self-sufficient in Christ's sufficiency; I am ready for anything and equal to anything through Him who infuses me with inner strength and confident peace.] [14] Nevertheless, it was right of you to share [with me] in my difficulties.

Job testified to what he feared has come to him. Manifestations don't lie. Being an entrepreneur because of fear of poverty will bring exactly that – ending up impoverished. The enterprise itself rather than be a channel of blessing becomes the road to deprivation. The counter-attack is simply getting out of poverty mentality. An entrepreneur God's way starts with the prophecy of God fulfilled in Christ.

2 Corinthians 8:9Amplified Bible (AMP)

[9] For you are recognizing [more clearly] the grace of our Lord Jesus Christ [His astonishing kindness, His generosity, His gracious favor], that though He was rich, yet for your sake He became poor, so that by His poverty you might become rich (abundantly blessed).

It is settled. The entrepreneur starts with abundance mentality. The abundance has been promised. All it takes is to walk the road where the abundance is easy pickings. The entrepreneur must stop trying to make money with a scarcity mindset and to start expressing creativity with an abundance mindset. In truth, lessons on how not to be broke must have been picked up at the financially destitute level. Otherwise, lessons unlearned are bound to be repeated. The lessons propel the entrepreneur to the next level where he discovers more lessons bringing him up to the moderately wealthy level unto the extremely rich level. The lesson keeps coming, the level gets higher, and the income grows bigger. Each new level offers new lessons as stepping stones to the next level.

Getting stuck at a certain level in all aspects already provided in redemption like health, relationships, finances, career, spiritual growth, or personal habits must not to be taken lightly. First and foremost, it may be normal to mere mortals but not to the believer who is a partaker of the divine nature. There is something terribly wrong that must be addressed immediately with impunity (since Satan is the cause of this!) and resolved right away. Wallowing in guild and throwing a pity party won't cut it. The grace of God is sufficient not just to endure for a brief moment but to overcome by the blood of the Lamb and the word of our testimony. The devil must not be given a foothold that can be a stronghold and end up a stranglehold.

The entrepreneur has the eternal Christ in his side. He is at His championship corner. He always leads in triumph. Nothing can stand in His way of being right and doing right.

Hebrews 13:5-6Amplified Bible (AMP)

5 Let your character [your moral essence, your inner nature] be free from the love of money [shun greed — be financially ethical], being content with what you have; for He has said, "I will never [under any circumstances] desert you [nor give you up nor leave

you without support, nor will I in any degree leave you helpless], nor will I forsake *or* let you down *or* relax My hold on you[assuredly not]!" ⁶So we take comfort *and* are encouraged *and* confidently say, "The Lord is my Helper [in time of need], I will not be afraid.

What will man do to me?"

Notice that although the promise of God echoed here from the Old Testament can be unilaterally applied to every situation, the original context is about finances. The entrepreneur is thus assured of complete success that must not cloud his character into the root of all evil – the love of money.

When all else seems to be getting nowhere, get away from it all. Go one on one with God totally without any distractions. Jesus did this with His apostles and He still wants to do this with all believers at any point in their lives. It is not just for ministers and preachers to come away with the Master regularly. Every believer should. Every believer pursuing God's plan should do this more often than others. Every entrepreneur must schedule this promptly at the onset of desert warning (that is sparseness of drought in hearing God regularly). God is with the entrepreneur to reach the next level. He is Author of such revelation of promotion.

Psalm 75:5-7 21st Century King James Version (KJ21)

5 Lift not up your horn on high; speak not with a stiff neck."

6 For promotion cometh neither from the east, nor from the west, nor from the south,

7 but God is the Judge: He putteth down one, and setteth up another.

Thus, if God is for the promotion of the entrepreneur, what would be holding the man from progressing? Paul has a marvelous advice to the Corinthians as he ends his communiqué with them. Full of love and yet rebuking and correcting, the Second Letter to the Corinthians is an epistle of an open heart from the apostle to the members of the church he started as a mission from God.

2 Corinthians 13:4-8 J.B. Phillips New Testament (PHILLIPS)

2-4 My previous warning, given on my second visit, still stands and, though absent, I repeat it now as though I were present—my coming will not mean leniency for those who had sinned before that visit and those who have sinned since. It will in fact be a proof that I speak by the power of Christ. The Christ you have to deal with is not a weak person outside you, but a tremendous power inside you. He was "weak" enough to be crucified, yes, but he lives now by the power of God. I am weak as he was weak, but I am strong enough to deal with you for I share his life by the power of God.

Why not test yourselves instead of me?

5-8 You should be looking at yourselves to make sure that you are really Christ's. It is yourselves that you should be testing, not me. You ought to know by this time that Christ is in you, unless you are not real Christians at all. And when you have applied your test, I am confident that you will soon find that I myself am a genuine Christian. I pray God that you may find the right answer to your test, not because I have any need of your approval, but because I earnestly want you to find the right answer, even if that should make me no real Christian. For, after all, we can make no progress against the truth; we can only work for the truth.

The Holy Spirit is the guarantee of this ever increasing rise to glory as God proposed and purposed. And God's purposes and plans cannot be thwarted. Promotion is destined for the entrepreneur. The lessons have to be learned. The next revelation and the subsequent manifestation must be built on the previous revelation already experienced and mastered. The die is cast. There is no turning back. The paths may grow steeper but the leg muscles previously used in climbing have now hardened to tackle even higher obstacles and jump over challenges.

Is the point to be accelerated from one level to the next? God forbid (that's original Greek text reaction)! The journey is the enjoyment. The arrival is just a bountiful bonus. The challenges hurdled, the victories savored, the setback endured are all forms of pleasures in varying degrees along the highway of adventures in faith in God. The focus as Christ was for the joy set before Him. The focus is Christ.

Hebrews 12:1-2 Amplified Bible, Classic Edition (AMPC)

12 Therefore then, since we are surrounded by so great a cloud of witnesses [who have borne testimony to the Truth], let us strip off *and* throw aside every encumbrance (unnecessary weight) and that sin which so readily (deftly and cleverly) clings to *and* entangles us, and let us run with patient

endurance *and* steady *and* active persistence the appointed course of the race that is set before us,

² Looking away [from all that will distract] to Jesus, Who is the Leader *and* the Source of our faith [giving the first incentive for our belief] and is also its Finisher [bringing it to maturity and perfection]. He, for the joy [of obtaining the prize] that was set before Him, endured the cross, despising *and* ignoring the shame, and is now seated at the right hand of the throne of God.

Is the point of life to immediately jump to a state of infinite health, wealth, relationship nirvana, and spiritual bliss? Of course and emphatically, it is not. The point is to enjoy the progression through various lessons that help the development and expansion of God consciousness. Whenever passing each level, the rewards are more lessons to catapult the entrepreneur to another level of more lessons. For believe it or not this is the way Jesus defined eternal life (not death means ending up in heaven).

Knowing God will take eternity. And it is not a quick fix instantaneous knowing of the Supreme Spirit. It is a progressive recognizing of the Invisible, Incomprehensible, and Inscrutable God as Pre-eminent over all. It is discovering that God first is 'bad theology.' It is God and God alone; no one even takes second place, even far, far, far second. Omnipotent, Omnipresent and Omniscient means the only All-Powerful, All-Present and All-Wise God.

Learning lessons one after the other and embracing the process of growth (though tedious along several patches of time) prevents stagnation, backsliding, falling away and disqualification.

Entrepreneurship is a rest from all the toils and travails of servile employment (for those anointed to be entrepreneurs). It is resting of the wisdom of God's ordained ways. It is resting on the promises of God who cannot lie. When the entrepreneur rests on present position and stop resisting, life becomes a beautiful

Chapter Six: Manifestations Don't Lie

thing, regardless of what level is currently on board experiencing. The next level is anticipated while still having immense fun right where the current level is. After all, hope cannot disappoint and hope is sure, joyous confident expectation of better things to come. And what is hoped for is to be clothed in exhilarating expectation of things yet unseen but sure to unfold; for no one hopes for what is already revealed and experienced. The hope is for the next better thing. It is not even termed 'best'. For if this is the best life now, there is no more expectation of anything better just a dreary feeling of sinking now to the abyss. That's why for some, the bottom is not a bad place to be since the next move is up.

'More than over comer' should no longer just be a catch phrase of the 'Christianese' language. To be more than an over comer means you had overcome something at least even the lowest type of hurdle. They may seem like bullies, obstacles, or dangers, but in truth their purpose is to make one a better player in the money game and to provide with an interesting experience worth the lesson learned.

Chapter Six: Manifestations Don't Lie

Chapter 7: The Final Conclusion

Confronting challenges develops God consciousness because as is the habit of most believers – when all else fails, there is God. Not a very good strategy but somehow a helpful one at the close or else the end shatters every -thing hoped for. Challenges help one discover new truths about self. They motivate to get moving and pursue goals. They make stronger. When one faces challenges, one discovers what kind of entrepreneur one really is. That's a priceless gift unmatched by any other.

To pinpoint the challenges at the current level, ask self, "What parts of this reality is currently being resisted not rested, and why? What parts of this reality is refused to be fully accepted?"

When about to go up a level through a challenging situation, what kind of emotions is felt? A sense of excitement, fun, and gratitude is good indicator. When one is not close to that level-up feeling, it means one is not yet ready to leave the current level.

Leveling up occurs only upon completion of the current level. This doesn't mean resolving to tie up every loose end. It simply means integrating the key lessons needed to learn.

If one is broke and wanting to experience financial abundance, has the entrepreneur learned the key lessons of being broke? Does the entrepreneur feeling taught enough of financial scarcity and immensely grateful To God that it can never happen in his life again?

If one is still struggling to figure out life's purpose and discovering a career direction, has the entrepreneur learned the bitter lessons of being directionless because of failing to hear God?

Proverbs 3:1-8Amplified Bible (AMP)

The Rewards of Wisdom

3 My son, do not forget my teaching,

But let your heart keep my commandments;

² For length of days and years of life [worth living]

And tranquility *and* prosperity [the wholeness of life's blessings] they will add to you.

³ Do not let mercy *and* kindness and truth leave you

[instead let these qualities define you];

Bind them [securely] around your neck,

Write them on the tablet of your heart.

4 So find favor and high esteem

In the sight of God and man.

5 Trust in *and* rely confidently on the Lord with all your heart

And do not rely on your own insight *or* understanding.

6 In all your ways

know *and* acknowledge *and* recognize Him,

And He will make your paths straight *and* smooth [removing obstacles that block your way].

7 Do not be wise in your own eyes;

Fear the Lord [with reverent awe and obedience] and turn [entirely] away from evil.

8 It will be health to your body [your marrow, your nerves, your sinews, your muscles—all your inner parts]

And refreshment (physical well-being) to your bones. The entrepreneur God's way can't move forward by not abhorring the current situation. No one became a saint by clinging on to be a sinner.

Matthew 9:13Amplified Bible (AMP)

13 Go and learn what this [Scripture] means: 'I desire compassion [for those in distress], and not [animal] sacrifice,' for I did not come to call [to repentance]the [self-proclaimed] righteous [who see no need to change], but sinners[those who recognize their sin and actively seek forgiveness]."

Luke 15:10Amplified Bible (AMP)

10 In the same way, I tell you, there is joy in the presence of the angels of God over one sinner who repents [that is, changes his inner self—his old way of thinking, regrets past sins, lives his life in a way that proves repentance; and seeks God's purpose for his life]."

Whenever one does resist the sinful reality, God's creative power to create a new creation in Christ is denied. The entrepreneur becomes powerless to progress bound by sin and deceived by Satan to resign self to the reality of remaining a sinner for eternity (as the devil is!).

Matthew 3:2 Amplified Bible (AMP)

2 "Repent [change your inner self—your old way of thinking, regret past sins, live your life in a way that

proves repentance; seek God's purpose for your life], for the kingdom of heaven is at hand."

Matthew 3:1 1Amplified Bible (AMP)

11 "As for me, I baptize you [a]with water because of [your] repentance [that is, because you are willing to change your inner self — your old way of thinking, regret your sin and live a changed life], but He (the Messiah) who is coming after me is mightier [more powerful, more noble] than I, whose sandals I am not worthy to remove [even as His slave]; He will baptize you [who truly repent] with the Holy Spirit and [you who remain unrepentant] with [b]fire (judgment).

Repentance is a must for every entrepreneur God's way. Acceptance of sinful reality leads to death. One must rebel at the poverty brought about by Satan into this world who boasted to Jesus he would give to Him the kingdoms if Jesus would bow to Satan. What preposterous hypocrisy! Satan is offering the bankrupt world system to the Creator of the universe as good and very good before Satan entered the physical realm. Satan is blocking man's progress to enjoy creation purposely created by God for man's enjoyment.

Chapter 7: The Final Conclusion

A block becomes a major problem when feels stunted and trapped in Satan's fake reality. One anxiously craves different experiences bored or frustrated with the doldrums of current level bogged down under Satan's clutches. That's a signal that the entrepreneur needs to turn towards Satan and trample on him and keep him under his feet. It's time to be strong in the Lord and the power of His might.

Move forward. Each move is the entrepreneur's faith in the goodness and guidance of God. The results become obvious as God-sent and God-given. Manifestations don't lie. God will always be for the entrepreneur God's way.

Other Books By the Author

- Mountaintop Boulevard - The Pilgrim's Journey into Bliss
- Don't Quit- Your Best Days Lie Ahead
- A Walk Into Eternity - An Inevitable Expedition of the Human Race
- Kingdom Attitude for Contagious Christian Living (ebook)

Contact Details for the Author:

Email: gmattoki@gmail.com

Facebook ID: www.facebook.com/gbenga.owotoki

Twitter: www.twitter.com/GbengaOwotoki